NATURE OF INDIAN CULTURE

NATURE OF INDIAN CULTURE

R.N. VYAS

CONCEPT PUBLISHING COMPANY, NEW DELHI 110059

ISBN 81-7022-388-1

First Published 1992

Published and Printed by
Ashok Kumar Mittal
Concept Publishing Company
A/15-16, Commercial Block, Mohan Garden,
NEW DELHI-110059
Phones : 25351460, 25351794
Fax : 091-11-25357103
E-mail : publishing@conceptpub.com

PREFACE

I FEEL pleasure in placing this small but significant volume in the hands of my readers.

Culture is fundamentally a unifying agency. It expresses itself in a communal life. An individual under its inspiration identifies himself with his tribe or community. But with the development of intelligence, culture has come to mean cultivation of those qualities which give a sense of nobility and oneness and destroy the germs of division and irrational distinctions. A man of culture rises above the limitations of nationality, religion, language, relationship or anything else of the kind. Ultimately, he identifies himself with the whole world. As is obvious, this development is not possible without the development of spiritual consciousness. Spirituality alone can lead to the rise of real culture which means total perfection and implies development of harmony of spirit, mind and body. This type of harmony is unattainable through scientific development alone.

Indian culture is sustained by its high spiritual outlook. The Brahman alone is the Real; hence, according to the most prominent Indian view, whatever exists in the universe is merely a manifestation of that Real alone through *Lila*. The Real is *Raso vai sah* (sweetness). The Lila is sweet. The universe too is an expression of this divine sweetness. One should try to understand this fact; and when once this fact is grasped, the walls of divisions and distinctions of every kind fall down and a sense of universal unison and oneness is attained.

It will be worthwhile to quote here the meaningful words of Aurobindo:

> "The whole aim of a great culture is to lift man up to something which at first he is not, to lead him to knowledge though he starts from an unfathomable ignorance, to teach him to live by his reason, though actually he lives much more by his unreason, by the law of good and unity, though he is now full of evil and discord, by a law

of beauty and harmony, though his actual life is a repulsive muddle of ugliness and jarring barbarisms, by some high law of his spirit, though at present he is egoistic, material, unspiritual, engrossed by the needs and desires of his physical being."

He adds:

"If a civilization has not any of these aims, it can hardly at all be said to have a culture and certainly in no sense a great and noble culture."

Indian culture has everything that is found in "a great and noble culture". It is rich in mathematics, astronomy, medicine, art, painting sculpture, literature, religion, philosophy and everything else that pertains to human life. What is worth noting is the fact that all these were basically inspired by high philosophical motives.

A fine synthesis of the physical and spiritual values has been achieved in Indian culture. And if a question is asked, "Which is more important – the spiritual or the mundane"? A clear answer is that spiritual life is nobler than a life devoted solely to power and enjoyment. The ultimate object is to help a man rise above the tumults of desires and aspirations and to help him, still further, to attain the acme of spiritual attainment. However, the world was never overlooked. The open declaration was "Enjoy life in a non-attached manner".

Not failure, but low aim is crime – says a wise dictum. If one tries to reach the spiritual perfection, one is bound to make one's world happier than what it is with a purely materialistic man. Our modern atomic weapons have brought humanity closest to total destruction. Adherence to Indian culture can pull humanity out of the present predicament because Indian mind holds the opinion that man is born a human animal but through culture he can be made a true human being *(janmana jayate shudro, sanskarat dwija ucchchate)*. Refinement of human nature is possible only through culture as understood and advocated by Indian thought.

A perusal of this book is expected to help a reader in understanding the nature of Indian culture, which is in fact universal or world culture. Social distances existing in the present world can be reduced and removed only through its philosophical touch and it alone can usher in a heaven of harmony and prosperity on this earth.

Rabindranath Tagore had stated in his Presidential address to the first session of the Indian Philosophical Congress in 1925,

> "The modern civilization is largely composed of *atmahano janah* who are spiritual suicides. It has lost its will for limiting its desires, for restraining its perpetual self-exaggeration. Because it has lost its philosophy of life, its art of living. Like poetasters it mistakes skill for power and realism for reality. . . . Today there is only a furious rage for raising numberless brick kilns in place of buildings. The great scheme of the master builder has been smothered under the heaps of brick dust. It proves the severance of *avidya* from her union with *vidya* giving rise to an unrhythymic power, ignoring all creative plan, igniting a flame that has heat but not light".

Only Indian culture can bring light in the present world of darkness. The present work tries to describe the important aspects of Indian culture within a few pages for the benefit of the modern reader who lacks patience and time to go through any bulky work.

The book, for the convenience of the reader, first deals with a description of the general nature of Indian culture, and then with some important topics like "Psychology in India", "Religious Philosophy of Kalidasa", "Indian Concept of Education for Rulers", "Voltaire and the Vedas", "India and the Peace Ideal", and "Aurobindo and Religion of Humanity" which try to offer Indian stand-points in matters of importance. The topics could not be fully elaborated because of the limited space. But they sufficiently reveal the basic nature of Indian thought in their respective spheres and inter-relation between religion and social service. I am of the opinion that the book offers enough knowledge about Indian culture to an interested reader.

I thank the publisher for taking interest in this work and for publishing it.

R.N. VYAS

Rabindranath Tagore had stated in his Presidential address to the first session of the Indian Philosophical Congress in [illegible]:

"The modern civilisation is [illegible] supposed [illegible] to be [illegible] [illegible] its [illegible] for [illegible] has lost its [illegible] ... [illegible] of living [illegible] mistake [illegible] today [illegible] for [illegible] in place of building. The [illegible] of the [illegible] has [illegible] the [illegible] of [illegible] from [illegible] power, ignoring all [illegible] that [illegible] light."

[illegible] which continues to live in the present [illegible]. The present work tries to describe the important aspects of Indian culture without [illegible] to the modern reader who [illegible] patience and interest to thoroughly study such [illegible].

This book, for the convenience of the reader, first deals with a description of the general features of Indian culture and then with some important topics like [illegible] in India, [illegible], Philosophy, [illegible] Indian Concept of Education, [illegible], [illegible] and the [illegible] and [illegible] of [illegible] in matters of [illegible] the [illegible] of the [illegible] nature of [illegible] in their respective spheres and [illegible] between [illegible] the opinion that the book [illegible] through [illegible] of [illegible].

[illegible] in this [illegible]

CONTENTS

CONTENTS

1

NATURE OF INDIAN CULTURE

CULTURE OCCUPIES an important place in human society. We daily hear of discussions concerning culture in the various forums, and people generally talk very eloquently about the cultural values. But despite this wide discussion and almost universal interest, it is difficult to say whether the concept of culture has been grasped properly. Hence, some consideration about the concept of culture is desirable.

Etymologically, the term culture signifies growth. In this very sense one talks about horticulture and agriculture. Scholars, however, differ as to the meaning of the term. Prof. Nirmal Kumar is of the opinion that culture consists of "certain aspects which are expressly meant to satisfy man's vital needs". According to P.A. Sorokin, Culture is the actual way of living and thinking expressed through human behaviour like art, literature, religion, etc. R.T. Lapiere states that culture is the totality of customs, traditions, institutions, etc., inherited by a people.

These eminent scholars of sociology, it will be noted, adopt a positivistic approach towards culture. But such a positive account of culture cannot do much good to humanity. We must rise above it, if we intend to grasp the true import of culture. Culture, in its elementary form, implies some kind of participation in the social life by an individual. But for a desirable standard of culture, it is necessary that an individual goes beyond a blind participation in social rites and rituals and cultivates those social virtues which persuade him to discard his brutish, selfish and ego-centric impulses for the attainment of genuine welfare of humanity. Participation in the social life is attained through the media of art, literature, education, religion, commerce, international relations. But a truly cultured person is not satisfied with this passive participation alone; he strives to become an embodiment of self-sacrifice and nobility.

If we analyse culture, we find that it consists of the following elements:

1. It is related to moral values.

2. It is concerned with perfection of individual character and conduct.
3. It tends to express itself through the channels of philosophy, history, art, religion, literature, etc.
4. It is not static and it changes to a certain extent according to the circumstances and the demands of the age.
5. Though it is subject to change, yet it has some elements which are eternal.

Thus culture has a peculiar nature. It contains both eternal as well as non-eternal elements.

In the modern period sometimes culture is divided into two categories, viz. culture proper and mass-and-popular culture. Norman Jacobs makes this very distinction and classification in his work *Culture for the Millions*. By the term culture is here meant the value of idealism accepted by society; and by the term "mass-culture" is meant the totality of desires inspired by the aptitudes of the masses. But, really speaking, this distinction is not justified. Mass-culture is merely an elementary form of culture and it has to grow in the form of idealistic culture, which is the soul of culture. The essence of culture is that it tries to bring about a process of unification in the midst of diversity existing in society. More than that, it inspires a community and its members to attain the ideal of moral perfection where the stinted self is so enlarged that the entire human society is brought in its sweep.

Culture is a "vaster music" which is produced when the individual interests are woven into a melody of social welfare in a spontaneous, smooth and beautiful manner. Unless the individual is enlarged and transformed truly and evolves into the Universal Man, true culture cannot come into being. Culture means raising "the pyramid of one's being as high as possible". According to Matthew Arnold the essence of culture consists in a certain type of "sweetness and light".

The *Oxford Dictionary* gives the following meaning of the term 'culture': "The training and refinement of mind, tastes and manners, the condition of being thus trained and refined, the intellectual side of civilization, the acquainting ourselves with the best." This makes it clear that culture has to be distinguished from civilization. Some people make the mistake of thinking that they are not separate. But this is obviously wrong. Civilization is concerned with the state of a society or community. One is civilized if one conforms to the civil standards of a community. It is concerned with the outward behaviour of a person. But culture is concerned with the mental refinement of a person. One may be civilized without being Cultured and, in the same way, one may be cultured without being civilized. But they should go together, because culture alone can give a constructive thrust to human civilization and progress.

That is why we find that there are different words like "arya" and "sabhya" in the Vedas. Arya is a cultured person, while "sabhya" is a person who can be a member of a "sabha". Civilization or "sabhyata" implies presence of certain social etiquette in a person. Civilization is thus material as it is concerned with the outward behaviour and customs of society. But culture is concerned with the inner being of a person. Civilizations differ because human communities differ from the standpoint of customs and rituals. But culture is universal in nature. Real culture can be mathematically expressed in the form of an equation:

$$1 \times 1 \times 1 \times 1 \ldots = 1$$

while civilization is based on distinction and difference. When human civilization imbibes the spirit of culture, our world will become a much better place than what it is at present.

In this context, it will be worthwhile to pay attention to the following words from the letter of T.E. Lawrence to Lionel Curtis, the Editor of the *Quarterly Review of Politics:* "Can there be profit, or truth in all these modes and sciences and arts of ours? The leisured world for hundreds, or perhaps thousands of years has been jealously working and recording the advance of each generation for the starting point of the next and here these masses are as animal, as carnal as their ancestors before Plato and Christ and Shelley and Dostoevsky taught and thought. In this crowd it's made startingly clear how short is the range of knowledge and what poor conductors of it ordinary humans are. You and I know; you have tried to tell all whom you reach and the end is here, a Cimmerian darkness with bog lights flitting wrongly through its gas."

Our modern world is facing a number of problems like exploitation, poverty, nepotism, war, etc., only because our civilization has not yet developed the cultural viewpoint.

Although culture is universal and it cannot be distinguished on the basis of nationality or continent, yet in some quarters it is confused with civilization, and often considered as interchangeable with civilization. When the term "culture" is so used, there appears some difference and distinction amongst the cultures of different nations. Thus there shall be difference between the American and the Soviet culture, the English and the French culture. But the outstanding difference will be between the Indian and the Western culture.

A Broad Distinction

History reveals that the Western culture is marked by intellectualism and materialism. On the other hand, Indian culture is spiritual and non-physical in nature. It should not be forgotten that this is a very broad distinction. But it does exist. For example, let us look at the meaning of "philosophy" and "darshana". The term "philosophy" means "love of knowledge", but the term "darshana" means "vision of truth". This tendency of philosophy is prevalent even in the modern times. Modern European philosophy has developed as an analysis of language. Thus the outstanding mark of the Western culture is its earthly nature. The other-worldly truth does not attract the West. But the remarkable quality of Indian culture is to love the "truth of truths", the Supreme Truth.

Yajnavalkya in the *Brihadaranyaka Upanishad* wanted to divide his property between his wives Katyayani and Maitreyi when he decided to renounce his household to enter *Sanyasa*. But Maitreyi said that she was interested in getting only that which could make here immortal. "Even if this whole earth replete with wealth be mine, venerable Sir, will it make me immortal?" The reply of Yajnavalkya was, "No, your life will be exactly like that of people well provided with materials, but there is no prospect of immortality through wealth". Maitreyi's reply is very revealing "What shall I do with that through which I cannot be immortal? Tell me, venerable Sir, of that alone which you know to be the means of immortality." Yajnavalkya replies that everything is dear because of the Self. "Verily all is dear not for the sake of all, my dear, but for the sake of the *Atman*." (*Brihadaranyaka Upanishad*: II-4-5)

Aurobindo states: "Indian culture recognizes the spirit as the truth of our being and our life as a growth and evolution of the spirit.[1] He says: "Man in the West has always been only an ephemeral creature of Nature. . . . Man in the Indian idea is a spirit veiled in the works of energy, moving to self-discovery, capable of Godhead."[2]

The entire edifice of Indian culture is based on the foundation of spirit. Her religion, art, literature, every thing has drawn inspiration from this spiritual outlook alone. The source books of Indian culture can be called "Shruti-Smriti-Puranokta", i.e. based on the *Shruti, Smriti* and *Puranas.*

The *Vedas* are known as *Shruti*, i.e. "direct from God" or revealed literature. They are considered to be "apaurusheya", i.e. not written by any man. Thus they are considered to be divine. Sayanacharya, the famous commentator of the Vedas, has stated that God created the whole universe out of the knowledge of the Vedas. It implies that Vedic knowledge existed even before the creation of mankind. The authority of the Vedas is not supposed to depend on any external authority. Their truth is verifiable by any spiritual aspirant in transcendental consciousness, the highest state of consciousness. There are four Vedas – *Rig Veda, Yajur Veda, Atharva Veda* and *Sama Veda.*

There are two distinct parts of every Veda: *Mantra* and *Brahmana (mantrabrahmanatmako vedah). Mantra* means panegyrics addressed to the deities. *Brahmana* means the detailed descriptions of the sacrifices to be performed to propitiate the deities.

A collection of *mantras* is called *samhita.* There are four such *samhitas*, viz. *Rik Samhita, Sama Samhita, Yajur Samhita* and *Atharva Samhita.* The *Bhagavata Purana* (1-4, 19-22) is of the opinion that this classification was made by Veda Vyasa.

We find three parts in every Veda, viz. *Samhita, Brahmana* and *Aryanaka. Aryanaka* is that portion of the Veda which is to be studied in *Aranya*, i.e. forest. This portion describes the acts that are to be pursued in the *Vanaprastha* stage of life. We shall see later on that *Vanaprastha* is one of the four *Ashramas* prescribed in Indian culture. The *Upanishads*, the philosophically most important statements, constitute the last portion of the *Aryanakas.* The *Upanishads* are known as the *Vedanta* because they appear as the last portion of the Vedas. We can categorize the contents of each of the four Vedas – *Rig, Sama, Yajur* and *Atharva* – in the following four parts: 1. *Samhitas*, 2. *Brahmanas*, 3. *Aryanakas*, 4. *Upanishads* We shall have an occasion to give the major ideas of the Vedas and the Upanishads later on.

Smritis are also important. The term "smriti" means memory. Thus *smritis* are those writings which are devised to fix in memory for use in practical life and conduct. They are the laws devised in the light of the basic teachings of the Vedas. There are many *Smritis*, but the Manu *Smriti* is the most important one. Manu states that his *Smriti* follows the Vedas,

yah kashcit kasyacit dharmo manuna parikirtitah
sa sarvo' bhihito vede sarvajnanamayo hi sah. (2-7)

The *Bhagavad Gita* too is considered to be a *Smriti*. The *Puranas* are also important sources of Indian culture. According to the *Vayu Purana*, the term *Purana* means "tradition or that which exists from the ancient times". The *Matsya Purana* describes the *Puranas* as "containing records of the past events". Thus the term Purana generally means an ancient narrative.

According to the traditional view, there are 18 *Maha* or major *Puranas* and 18 or 20 *Upa* or minor *Puranas*. The *Puranas* are not independent creations. They serve the purpose of propagating the teaching of the Vedas in a popular manner. The *Chhandogya Upanishad* calls them the fifth Veda. According to the *Mahabharata*, whosover approaches the Vedas without first studying the *Itihasa* and the *Puranas* frightens the Vedas.

The *Puranas* were written to explain and elucidate the high philosophy and religion of the Vedas and the Upanishads to the ordinary public in an easy and comprehensible language and style.

Apart from the above-mentioned literature, the *Ramayana* and the *Mahabharata* too are very important from the standpoint of an understanding of the Indian culture. The *Ramayana* is the story of Rama's life and his battle against *Ravana* who was the symbol of wickedness. The *Mahabharata* is the story of the conflict between the Pandavas and the Kauravas. The Pandavas stood for righteousness while the Kauravas for the evil.

Swami Vivekanand has presented the importance of these two great works in the following words:

> "The internal conflicts between righteousness and filial affection in the mind of the God-fearing yet feeble old blind King Dhritarashtra; the majestic character of the grandsire Bhishma; the noble and virtuous nature of the royal Yudhishthira and the other four brothers, as mighty in valour as in devotion and loyalty; the peerless character of the women, the stately queen Gandhari, the loving mother Kunti, the ever devoted and all-suffering Draupadi – these and hundreds of other features of this epic and of the Ramayana have been the cherished heritage of the whole Hindu

world for the last several thousands of years, and form the basis of its thoughts and of its moral and ethical ideas".[3]

The *Ramayana* is the first poem of the world. Valmiki who became a sage renouncing his old unethical habits once saw, amid the branches of a tree, a pair of doves wheeling and billing. But just then an arrow whisked past him and buried itself in the body of the male bird. As the dove fell to the ground, his mate whirled about him in deep grief. Valmiki then saw the hunter and exclaimed his righteous anger,

> "For endless years to come, O hunter, never shall thy soul find peace,
> Since for love itself thou wouldst not from thy cruel slaying cease."

The basic foundation of Indian culture has been provided by the above- mentioned works. Their influence has penetrated the very being of Indian culture.

Great thinkers, poets, law-givers, kings, artists and others who flourished in India, were inspired primarily by these works alone. This influence worked sometimes directly, sometimes indirectly. But it did work. The spiritual aspect of the Indian culture distinguishes it from the Western culture. Perhaps this spirituality of culture gave India that strength which could not be defeated by any foreign invasion. One Indian poet has pointed out to this very fact when he wrote, "There is something in us because of which our culture and existence still persist, while many ancient cultures have long ceased to exist and are present only in the pages of history." The ideal of Indian culture has been from its very dawn to bring peace and prosperity to the entire world through cordial love and affection. Spirit is by nature immortal. It is but natural, therefore, that spiritual culture of India too is immortal and eternal (*Sanatana*).

REFERENCES

1. *Sri Aurobindo on India*, p.9.
2. ibid. 18.
3. *Complete Works of Vivekananda*, Vol. IV, pp.96-7.

2

BULWARKS OF INDIAN CULTURE

INDIAN CIVILIZATION can be considered to have begun in the pre-historic period. It started in the Palaeolithic Age or the Old Stone Age. Archaeological excavations carried out in Mohen-jo-daro and Harappa in 1922 revealed that there existed a remarkable civilization beside the Indus. That is why it has been given the name of the Indus Valley Civilization. But no written records of this civilization are available. However, it is clear that it was a remarkably flourishing civilization, because the relics indicate the existence of good buildings made of bricks, arts and crafts, trade and commerce, and religious institutions like the worship of God Shiva. This civilization was destroyed in course of time.

For a proper understanding of Indian culture, we must begin from the Vedic period.

We have already mentioned that there are four Vedas. The oldest and the most important Veda is the *Rig Veda*. The Veda was originally one. But, as per tradition, Veda Vyasa classified it in four books called the *Rig Veda*, the *Sama Veda*, the *Yajur Veda* and the *Atharva Veda*. The *Rig Veda* is the oldest book of the world. It has been divided into 10 *mandalas* or circles and contains 1,028 hymns. It is actually a collection of hymns composed by different seers of truth *(Rishis)*.

We shall have here a glimpse of the social life prevailing at the time of the *Rig Veda*. It will indicate that simplicity characterized the life of the people living in that period.

It appears that people resided then in that part of India which is called the Punjab at present, because the term "Sapta-Sindhu", the land of seven rivers, is clearly mentioned. The repeated use of the term proves that the hymns of the *Rig Veda* were composed in the land of the modern Indus and its tributaries.

The *Soma* plant occupied a very significant place in the *Rig Vedic* society. It was used for sacrificial purposes as well as for preparing a drink. As the *Some* grew only in the mountainous region, we can conclude that the seers of the *Rig Veda* mostly lived in the vicinity of the mountains. We come across statements that lead to this conclusion. "This *Soma*, clad with leaves and foliage, dwells on the central mountains of the earth." (*Rig Veda* IX.82.3) "O *Soma*, thy birthplace is in the heaven. Thence thy limbs were cast on the mountains, where they have grown up as trees." (RV IX.79.4) "These *Soma* creepers, having grown in the mountainous region, are being distilled on sacrificial ground, which is the meeting place of the gods." (RV IX.46.1).

Even though the Aryan people of the Rigvedic period were simple, their society was not entirely free from conflict. "All around us are the Dasyu tribes; they do not perform sacrifices; they have no faith; their rites are different." (RV X.22.8)

Therefore, we come across battle hymns too. The art of fighting was quite developed. The chief weapon was the bow and arrow. We come across a statement that proves it. "The blacksmith, having made arrows with the help of dry wood and feathers of birds – as well as shining stones for the points – looks for some wealthy purchaser." (RV IX.112.2) "We salute the great goddess arrow, which is poisoned, whose head is destructive, whose mouth is of iron." (RV VI.75.15)

The horses were trained for the battle. The cattle was the chief wealth of the people who were mostly agriculturists. *Pushan*, one of the earliest gods, was the protector of cattle. *Dhayman* (rice) was the chief produce.

"The ploughs are being arranged", states one of the hymns, and adds, "The labourers are taking out the yokes. The wise people are reciting praises unto gods. Prepare reservoirs of drinking water for the cattle, tie up the leathern strings; let us draw water from this fine pit with an inexhaustible supply of water."

Cows and horses were used for agricultural purposes. The names of other domestic animals like buffaloes, sheep and goats too occur in the *Rig Veda*. The training of elephants was also known. Gifts of the animals was considered very auspicious. One hymn states, "King Kasu of the Cheri dynasty gave away hundred camels and ten thousand cows." (RV VIII.5.37)

The use of cloth was prevalent. "He (Pusha) weaves cloth of wool and he washes cloth." Use of ornaments of gold too was prevalent. Use of iron was quite popular. Carpentry, navigation and commerce too flourished at that time.

Monarchical system of government was popular. Many kings are mentioned. Divadasa and Sudasa seem to be very popular kings. But the post of king was not hereditary. Sacrificial activity was prevalent. women were given due honour. We come across the names of three prominent women, Ghosha, Apala and Vishvavara, in the Vedic hymns. "Vishvavara, with her face turned to the east and with the pot of sacrificial offerings in her hand, is proceeding towards fire singing praises unto gods" states one of the hymns.

In the beginning, sacrifice was a simple affair. But later an it became somewhat complicated. One hymn states, "One (*hota*) cooperates with us by reciting the *mantras* profusely, another *(udgata)* sings the *Saman* in the *Gayatri* metre, brahma explains the *Jata-Vidya* (order of sacrifices), another *(adhwaryu)* again performs the various rites of sacrifice one by one." (RV X.71.11)

The caste system was not known to that period. People followed any profession of their liking. One hymn states, "Different persons among us have different avocations. The carpenter saws wood, the physician looks after patients, the priest seeks persons desirous of performing sacrifices." (RV IX.112.1) One priest prays for a warrior son. The son of a descendant of the King Paruchpeda was a rishi and the author of many hymns. In one family, there used to be followers of different professions as is clear from the following hymn: "I am a composer of hymns. My son is a physician, and my mother a grinder of fried barley. We are of different professions." (RV IX.112.3)

Religious Ideas

We come across a very simple concept of religion in the Rig Vedic period. People saw divinity in the various aspects of nature. They called the deity the way they liked. But mostly these deities were personifications of nature's phenomena. The principal names of the deities that occur in the Rig Veda are: Indra, Agni, Soma, Vayu, Surya, Mitra, Varuna, Vishnu, Usha, the twin Ashwins, Pusha, Rudra, Prajapati, Yama, Parjanya, Aryama, Marutas, Brihaspati, Saraswati, Aditi, Adityas, Ribhus, Ila, Twashta, Savita, Indrani, Varunani, Agneyi, Vasus, Matarishva, Vaishwanara and Bharati.

Generally it was recognized that there are 33 deities as is evident from the following hymn:

> "O ye Devas, destroyers of enemies and worthy of the sacrifices of men, the sons of Manu, you are thirty-three in number and have

thus been praised." (RV VIII.30.2)

Apparently, there appears to be a diversity of gods. But the worthy seers knew that ultimately there is only one Real. The following hymns make this clear:

> "Men think that they have drunk Soma, when they press the vegetable. But no one can drink the Soma whom the sages know." (RV X85.3)

> "He (Varuna) knows the path of birds that fly through
> heaven and sovran of the sea,
> He knows the ships that are thereon.
> True to his holy law, he knows the
> twelve moons with their progeny.
> He knows the moon of later birth,
> He knows the pathway of the wind,
> the spreading high and mighty wind.
> He knows the gods who dwell above Varuna,
> True to holy laws, sits down among his people;
> He most wise, sits there, to govern." (RV I.25.7-10)

Wise seers realized that "the great might of the Devas is one" and they expressed their intuitive truth by declaring, "They call him Indra, Mitra, Varuna, Agni and the heavenly noble-winged Garutman; sages call the one reality by many names. Agni, Yama, Matarishva." (RV I.164.46) "They (the earth and the heavens) are not all; there is another above them. He is the creator, He preserves the earth and heavens, He is the lord of food." (RV X.31.8)

It appears that the wise seers of the Rig Veda knew that the ultimate truth is one, but they allowed everybody to give this truth the name of his liking. This tendency is called henotheism. A person would worship Surya and would see the supreme truth in it alone, the other would see the supreme in his god Agni. Everybody was sure that ultimately there is only one truth that exists. But this truth was not recognized by all. Indians always believed in Adhikari-bheda or the difference between the grasping ability of persons. Hence the ultimate truth was not clear to every person. But as a person made a little progress, he realized that "the great might of the Devas is one".

This tendency found its full expression in the Upanishads which are the last portions of the Vedas.

Human intelligence plays its vital role in the recognition of truth. That is why the seer of the *Rig Veda* prays,

> "Let us meditate on the adorable light of the great *Savita*, who inspires us with intelligence." (RV III.62.10)

Those who consider Indian philosophy other-worldly or world-negating should go through the *Rig Veda*. They shall find there abundant love for life. People loved life, wealth, health and such other things which are considered valuable in life. But the Indian mind could transcend material attitude of life even in the *Rig Vedic* period. End of the body is not the end of the soul. There is a world of immortality for the spirit. The seer sings:

> "O, *Pavamana*, place me in that deathless, undecaying world
> Wherein the light of heaven is set, and ever-lasting
> lustre shines." (RV IX.113.7)
> "Make me immortal in that realm of where
> dwells the king, Vivaswah's son." (RV IX.113.8)

In the *Yajur Veda* too basic unity of human life has not been forgotten. For example, we may see the following statement: "Give lustre to our *Brahmanas*; set lustre to our *Kshatriyas*, lustre to *Vaishyas* and *Shudras*; give, through lustre, lustre unto me." (YV XVIII.18)

The ultimate truth is one. This was the view of the seers of the *Yajur Veda* too. For example, we can consider the following hymn: "*Agni* is *'tat'*; the *sun* is *'tat'*; *Vayu* and *Chandramas* are *'tat'*; the Bright is *'tat'; Brahma* is *'tat'*, those waters, and *Prajapati* are *'tat'*." (YV XXXII)

> "Enveloped by the Lord must be this all-each that moves on earth." (YV XI.1)
> "We have attained the light and grown immortal; we have gone up from earth to heaven, have found the gods and heaven and light." (YV VIII.52)

The spirit of the *Rig Veda* can be seen even in the *Atharva Veda*. But it also abounds in hymns of charms and incantations against diseases and demons. This only indicates that love for life was abundantly present in the people of that period. Not only there was love for life, there was love for the earth too. There is an inspiring ode to the earth *(bhumi)*. It begins with,

> "On whom the ocean and the rivers, and the waters, on whom food and corn lands came into being, on whom this all that breathes, moves, and is active, let the earth set us in first" (RV XIII.13).

The Brahmanas generally support ceremonialism. After all society consists of all types of people. Even those persons who are fond of ceremonies are a part of society. Even in modern period ceremonialism is prevalent in some form or the other. We find evidence of this fact in churches, gurudwaras, temples and, in fact, in every religious place. According to the *Brahmanas*, even the gods are controlled by the sacrifices.

"The sacrifice fled away from the gods. The gods called out after it, 'Listen to us, come back to us'. It replied 'so be it', and returned to the gods and with what had thus returned to them, the gods worshipped and by worshipping with it they became the gods they are bow." (*Shatpatha Brahmana* V.2.6) Sacrifice is sometimes given a very lofty meaning when it is declared that sacrifice is *Vishnu (Vishnuvai yajnah)*.

However, the cultimation of absolutistic thought is found in the Upanishads. The ideas about the Supreme Truth are present in the Vedas too. But their full expression is found in the *Upanishads*. It is in the fitness of things that the Upanishads constitute the last portions of the Vedas because such thoughts can emerge only after a thorough critical speculation.

The Upanishads are termed the *Vedanta* because they are, really speaking, the culmination of human thought. The outstanding feature of the Upanishads is that they strongly oppose the ritualistic attitude and declare that emancipation can come only through knowledge. They contain a very bold speculation about the nature of the ultimate reality and conclude that there is only one ultimate reality which has been termed the *Atman* or the *Brahman* by the Upanishads.

The Upanishads are supposed to be 108 in number. In length they range from a few hundred to thousands of words. Some are in prose, some in verse. They are the speculations of a number of thinkers. All of them are not of equal importance. The *Brahma Sutra* has tried to bring about a coherence in the teachings of the different Upanishads.

And the first systematic study of the Upanishads was undertaken by Shankaracharya. He wrote a commentary on the *Brahma-sutras* and quoted from the following *Upanishads* (the figures in brackets indicate the number of quotations): 1. *Chhandogya* (809), 2. *Brihadaranyaka* (565), 3. *Taittiriya* (142), 4. *Mundaka* (129), 5. *Katha* (103), 6. *Kaushitaki* (88), 7. *Swetashwatara* (52), 8. *Prashna* (31), 9. *Aitareya* (22), 10. *Jabala* (13), 11. *Mahanarayana* (9), 12. *Isha* (8), 13. *Paingi* (6), 14. *Kena* (5). But Shankaracharya actually wrote separate commentaries on the following Upanishads alone: *Isha, Kena, Katha, Prashna, Mundaka, Mandukya, Taittiriya, Aitareya, Chhandogya, Brihadaranyaka* and *Swetashwatara.*

Therefore, these are the most important Upanishads. and the message of the Upanishads is so sublime that the scholars of the East as well as the West are unanimous about the greatness of these works.

It is to be remembered that the Upanishads are actually the collections of insights of the seers. There is no attempt to give them any systematic form. Hence, sometimes a reader may think that there are certain inconsistencies in the statements. But these inconsistencies are merely the expressions of the experiences of seers at different levels of spiritual development. Ultimately, these contradictions are merged in the unity of the absolute.

For example, let us consider the following passages:

> "In the heart of all things, of whatever there is in the universe, dwells the Lord." (*Isha Up.* I)
>
> "The Imperishable is the Real. As sparks innumerable fly upward from a blazing fire, so from the depths of the Imperishable arise all things. To the depths of the Imperishable they again return."
>
> "Self-luminous is that Being, and formless. He dwells within all and without all. He is unborn, pure, greater than the greatest, without breath, without mind."
>
> "From Him are born breath, mind, the organs of sense, ether, air, fire, water, and the earth, and He binds all these together.
>
> "Heaven is His head, the sun and moon His eyes, the four quarters His ears, the revealed scriptures His voice, the air His breath, the universe His heart. From His feet came the earth. He is the innermost self of all." (*Mundaka Up.* II.1.1-4)

The Brihadaranyaka tells us that "for the illumined mind the all is dissolved in the self."

Thus, according to the Upanishads, the ultimate reality is the *Brahman*. The *Brahman* is also known as the *Atman*. There is no difference between the two; they are the two names of one reality. "That art thou." *(tat tvam asi)*.

We shall have an opportunity to turn to this topic once again when we discuss the nature of Indian philosophy. Suffice it to state that according to the Upanishads, the apparent multiplicity is an illusion. The Self is the only Real.

It is worth noting that all Indian thoughts of philosophy have emanated from the Upanishads, because the latter happen to be the store-house of different thoughts. Even the heterodox systems of Indian philosophy like the *Charvaka*, the *Jaina* and the *Bauddha* have drawn their inspiration from the Upanishads alone. That is why Indian philosophical systems have some common features. We need not dwell at length on this point due to the limited objective of the present work.

The Epics and the Puranas

Indian culture was shaped by the *Itihasa* and the Puranas too. The *Ramayana* and the *Mahabharata* are considered to be *Itihasa*, while the Puranas consist of *Maha Puranas* and *Upa Puranas*. The study of *Itihasa* and the Puranas has been considered necessary for the correct interpretation of the Vedas. The epics and the Puranas constitute an important source of cultural history of India. In fact, *Itihasa* and the Puranas are considered to be the fifth Veda, i.e. they are as important as the other Vedas. And this view is quite correct because ordinary people derive their knowledge of Indian culture from these very sources. The Vedas and the Upanishads are no doubt very important, but they are not very popular with the common man of India. For him, the Ramayana and the *Mahabharata* are more important, and he derives his ideals from them, draws inspiration from them.

The Mahabharata

According to Panini, "Bharata" signifies "the battle of the Bharatas". Accordingly, the *Mahabharata* means "the great narrative of the battle of the Bharatas". The *Mahabharata* itself tries to explain the meaning of the term *Mahabharata* – the work is given the name of the *Mahabharata* on account of its greatness, enormous size and weightiness, implying that it outweighs the Vedas and other scriptures *(mahatvad bharavattvaccha mahabharatamuchyate).*

But the most apt reason for the name is that "it is called *Mahabharata* because in it is narrated the great life-story of the Bharatas." The Bharatas are mentioned as a warrior tribe in the Rig *Veda.* In the *Mahabharata* this very nucleus provided the basis of the great epic. The bulk became enlarged because of the addition of legends, myths, didactic material, fables and poetry. The result is that it is at once a *Kavya, Shastra, Shruti*, law, philosophy, etc. In fact the *Mahabharata* is an encyclopaedia. It contains everything that can be called important. The *Mahabharata* itself confirms it by saying that whatever is present in it may be found elsewhere; what is not present here cannot be got anywhere else *(yadihasti tadanyatra yannehasti na tatkvachit).* Indian tradition rightly declares that Vyasa has touched everything under sun *(vyasochcchi shtam jagatsarvam).*

Veda Vyasa, the son of Parashara and Satyavati, is supposed to be the author of this great work. According to the story found in the *Mahabharata* itself, he was the procreator of the sons Dhritarashtra and Pandu from Vichitravirya's childless widows Ambika and Ambalika by *niyoga*, a practice prevalent at that time. After composing the poem, Vyasa taught it to his son Shuka and other deserving students.

The *Mahabharata* is a voluminous work. According to one opinion, it contains 100,000 stanzas. The *Mahabharata* itself mentions that Narada recited this poem to Gods, Devala recited it to *manes*, Shuka recited it to *Gandharvas* and demons, and Vaishampayana, who was the pupil of Vyasa, recited it to mortal beings. The tradition states that as it was not possible for an ordinary human being to write such an enormous work, god Ganesha accepted to be the scribe. But he put the condition that he would not stop writing even for a moment. Sage Vyasa thereupon stated that although this condition was acceptable to him, Ganesha should not write anything unless he comprehended it. Accordingly, Vyasa put a number of riddles *(kuta shlokas)* in the epic. These riddles puzzled even Ganesha. The number of such riddles is supposed to be 8,800.

Suta (Sauti or Ugrashravas) heard the narration told by Vaishampayana to Janamejaya and gave it out as the *Mahabharata* to the sages assembled in the Naimisha forest during Shaunaka's sacrifice.

There is no unanimity about the date of composition of this work.

But the importance of the *Mahabharata* for understanding the nature of Indian culture is acceptable to all the people of India. It may be noted that the celebrated *Bhagvad Gita*, which is respected by all the Indians, is a part of the *Mahabharata*. The *Mahabharata* represents a whole literature rather than a single homogeneous work. It is a veritable treasure house of Indian lore, both secular and religious. The story of the *Mahabharata* may briefly be mentioned here.

Dhritarashtra became king after the death of his brother Pandu. He brought up the five sons of Pandu with his own sons who were one hundred in number. As they grew up, the Pandavas, i.e. the sons of Pandu, distinguished themselves for their valour and love for righteousness. But this produced a sense of jealousy in Duryodhana, the eldest son of Dhritarashtra. He conspired many times along with his brothers and friends to kill the Pandavas. On one occasion the Pandavas were invited to visit with their mother Kunti a distant town named Varnavata on the plea that a religious festival was being held there. There they were accommodated in a palace built, on Duryodhana's instructions, of inflammable materials. But the Pandavas were warned of the plot by a good man; and therefore, they managed to escape before the house was set afire. When Duryodhana and his brothers learnt that the palace has been reduced to ashes, they thought that all obstacles were removed from their path.

But the Pandavas had actually fled to the forest along with their mother, where they lived in the guise of Brahmins. They had to face many difficulties, but their fortitude, physical strength and extraordinary valour helped them in overcoming all of them. By chance, during this time, they heard of the approaching marriage festival *(Swayamvara)* of princess Draupadi. Kings and princes were to assemble at the court of her father Drupada, and the princess was to choose for her husband, one among them who could string the unique bow, and pierce a difficult target. The Pandavas decided to go to the ceremony in the garb of Brahmins.

The day came when the suitors gathered from all parts of India to try their luck and win the hand of the beautiful princess. Among these suitors was Duryodhana too. One after another they tried their skill, but none could even lift the bow, let alone string it. Of the five Pandava brothers – Yudhishthira, Bhima, Arjuna, Nakula and Sahadeva, Arjuna was a great archer. He then stood up, quietly approached the arena, and with ease lifted the bow, strung it and hit the target. Thereafter, Draupadi, the princess, put the garland of flowers around Arjuna's head, accepting him as her husband. However, the other kings and princes gathered there could not bear the thought of a princess being won by a poor Brahmin, so they tried to prevent the marriage by force of arms. The five brothers fought all these warriors, won the battle, and carried away the bride.

The five brothers then came back to their home along with Draupadi. Their home was in a forest and they were living on alms. They told their mother, Kunti, in jest: "Mother, today we have brought a wonderful gift." Kunti was lost in some thought and, therefore, even without looking at the gift, she said, "Enjoy the gift in common, my children, all of you." Then, seeing the princess, she cried out: "Oh, what have I said, "But nothing could be done, because for those dutiful sons, mother's word could not be disregarded. Thus, as the luck would have it, Draupadi became the common wife of all the Pandava brothers.

Dhritarashtra, the king, and his jealous sons now learnt that the Pandavas were not only alive, but they had also married Draupadi and had thus formed a strong alliance with a powerful neighbouring king. Though Duryodhana had some fresh plots in his mind to kill the Pandavas, he was advised by his wise counsellors to call the Pandavas back and offer them half of his kingdom. The king could not ignore the advice of elderly and responsible persons like Bhiṣhma and Vidura. Accordingly, the kingdom was divided. Duryodhana took possession of the richer eastern portion, with its ancient capital Hastinapura on the Ganges, and Yudhishthira, the eldest of the Pandavas, was given the western portion of the kingdom, which was then a wilderness.

The Pandavas were wise and strong. They cleared a space in the forest and built a beautiful city which was given the name of Indraprastha. When their kingdom was thus happily established they made plans for holding the *Rajasuya Yajna* (Imperial Sacrifice), that witnessed the crowning ceremony of Yudhishthira, the eldest Pandava, as king. However, before this sacrifice, the Pandavas attacked Jarasandha, who held captive many of other kings with the intention of killing them, and defeated him. This attack was made at the suggestion of Shrikrishna, the cousin brother of the Pandavas. To the Imperial Sacrifice came the liberated kings with rich offerings. Other kings also came to pay their tribute. Dhritarashtra and his sons, having been duly invited, were present. Shri Krishna, who was held in high esteem by the Pandavas, also attended the ceremony. Utmost respect was paid to him by giving him the foremost honour as the most worshipable person of the age. Yudhishthira was crowned amidst great rejoicing.

The most splendid crowning of Yudhishthira made Duryodhana all the more jealous. He, therefore, planned with the active guidance of Shakuni, his maternal uncle, to wrest the kingdom of Pandavas in a deceitful manner. A scheme was prepared. Yudhishthira was invited to a game of dice in Hastinapura. He could not decline the invitation as, in those times, no king could customarily decline such an offer. Hence, Yudhishthira accepted the invitation albeit very reluctantly. Crafty Shakuni knew how to manipulate the game, and Yudhishthira was defeated. The result was that Yudhishthira lost everything – his kingdom, his brothers, himself, and even his queen Draupadi – in the game.

The plot of Duryodhana and Shakuni was thus successful. The Pandavas were now completely at the mercy of Duryodhana, who used the opportunity to heap insults on the Pandavas and ill-treated Draupadi.

However, Dhritarashtra intervened, set the brothers free along with Draupadi and returned Yudhishthira's kingdom.

But Duryodhana wanted to insult and destroy the Pandavas. He, therefore, hatched another plot. Once again he challenged Yudhishthira to play a game of dice. This time Duryodhana took the permission of his father too. The condition of the play was very strange and shocking. The loser would have to give up his kingdom and retire to the forest for 12 years, and thereafter live unrecognized in a city for one year, and if he were found out during that year, the same term of exile would have to be endured once again. As was expected, this time too Yudhishthira lost. Therefore he had to go to the forest along with his brothers and Draupadi for the stipulated period. There they dwelt for 12 years, practising many virtues and austerities and performing many deeds of bravery. The part of the epic dealing with this period is replete with interesting stories and is studded with great ethical and spiritual teachings.

Once, while wandering in the forest, the Pandavas felt very thirsty, whereupon Yudhishthira sent one of his brothers Nakula in search of water. Nakula found a crystal lake, but as he was about to drink from it, he heard a voice say: "Stop, child, first answer my questions, and then drink water." But Nakula being very thirsty did not care for the warning, drank water and dropped down dead.

As he failed to return, Sahadeva was sent to find out Nakula and water. He too came to the same lake and met the same fate. Arjuna and

Bhima too had to face the same fate.

At last Yudhishthira came to the lake and saw the dead bodies of his four beloved brothers. When he was lamenting for his brothers, he heard a voice, "Yudhishthira, my child, answer my questions, and your grief and thirst will be over."

"I will answer your questions according to my understanding" replied Yudhishthira." "Ask of me."

The voice that spoke to Yudhishthira was the voice of *Dharma* (Virtue) which had assumed the form of a crane.

Q. "What is the path to heaven?"
A. "Truthfulness."
Q. "By what means does one find happiness?"
A. "By right conduct."
Q. "By subduing what do men escape grief?"
A. "By subduing their minds."
Q. "When is a man loved?"
A. "When he is without vanity."
Q. "Of all the strange things in the world what is the most strange?"
A. "That no one, though he sees people dying all around him, believes that he will die."
Q. "By what path does one reach religion?"
A. "By argument it cannot be reached. Of scriptures and doctrines there are many, but they avail not. The path to religion is that which is trødden by the saints."

Dharma, thereupon, was pleased, revealed himself to Yudhishthira and brought back to life his dead brothers.

As *Dharma* knew that the thirteenth year of the exile to which the Pandavas were doomed had just begun and that it was required of them that they should live in a city unrecognized, he helped them all to change their appearance and advised them to go to the kingdom of Virat. Many were the incidents that took place there during the year in which, disguised, they served the king of Virat, but their identity was discovered only at its close. In this way all the conditions of the wager were fulfilled.

Then Yudhishthira asked Duryodhana to restore to him his kingdom. But Duryodhana paid no attention to it. Yudhishthira then said that he would be content if only he and his brothers were each given a village. But even this proposal was rejected by the evil-minded

Duryodhana. "Without a struggle," he roared, "I will not given even so much land as can be covered by the point of a needle."

Elders of the hostile families did their utmost to settle the quarrel, even Shrikrishna tried his level best, but Duryodhana was adamant. Under the circumstances, preparations for the inevitable war were started.

Shrikrishna, though both sides desired his help, would take no active part in the fight, but he gave his army to Duryodhana and offered himself as charioteer to Arjuna on the latter's request.

The war was going to cause a holocaust. The neighbouring kings were also drawn into the conflict, and even the distant ones participated. In other words, entire India became involved in the war, which was fought on the plains of Kurukshetra. But when the opposing armies were to begin the conflict, Arjuna became baffled about the desirability of the conflict because he thought he was going to commit a great sin by killing his kinsmen and the teachers who were to fight on the side of Duryodhana. At that crucial hour Shrikrishna, who has been accepted as an *avatara* of God, gave an immortal teaching to Arjuna, which is known as the *Bhagavad Gita*.

The battle lasted for 18 days, and finally when Duryodhana was killed, it ended in favour of the Pandavas.

Yudhishthira thus became the undisputed emperor of India and ruled for 36 years. After him Parikshita, the grandson of Arjuna, became the emperor because the Pandavas along with Draupadi retired to the Himalayas. There, free from the worldly worries, they practised austerities.

The epic ends with the story of their great journey to the abode of God. All the Pandavas and Draupadi set out together; but one by one all fell down dead on the way, because they were not sufficiently pure to be able to enter heaven in their human bodies. However, Yudhishthira was able to reach heaven in his human body because he had no fault. Awaiting him there were queen Draupadi, his four brothers and others, relatives and friends who had died on earth. Thus lost relatives were united once again in heaven. We may narrate here one incident that deserves a mention. Yudhishthira is accompanied on his last journey by his faithful dog Dhruba.

When, together, they reached heaven, Yudhishthira is granted admission, but not Dhruba. "Without Dhruba," declares Yudhishthira, "I will not enter." Thereupon Yudhishthira is allowed to enter with his dog Dhruba.

The incident shows the utmost purity of Yudhishthira's heart. The *Mahabharata* contains innumerable statements about morality and practical wisdom. We may quote a few here:

> "Treat others as you yourself shall like to be treated."
> "Do nothing to your neighbour which hereafter you would not have your neighbour do to you."
> "He who is always a friend of others and by his word, thought, and deed is continually engrossed in doing good to others, he alone knows the meaning of dharma."
> "Alms-giving is the way to fame, truthfulness is the way to heaven, right conduct is the way to happiness. The best of gains is the gaining of health, and the best of happiness is contentment."
> "There is no greater virtue than kindness. They who have their mind under control never come to grief. Friendship with the holy never ages."
> "He who gives up vanity is loved by all. He who gives up anger never grieves. He who gives up greed becomes happy."
> "Kindness is desiring happiness for all. Straightforwardness is mental poise. Holy is he who is kind to all. Wicked is he who is cruel."

There is an incident in the *Mahabharata*, Bhishma who was one of the most valiant fighters and grand old man of both Pandavas and Kauravas was wounded. He was lying on a bed of arrows waiting for the auspicious time for breathing his last. Shrikrishna asked the Pandavas to learn the rules of wisdom and culture from him. Bhishma gives a sermon on many things, from the duties of a monarch to the secrets of philosophy. Some of them may be mentioned here.

> "Man should always worship God with devotion – this I consider the greatest of all truths."
> "The blessed ones who love the Lord and are devoted to Him are free from anger, malice, avarice, and evil thoughts."
> "Meditating on thee, O Krishna, the energy of youth has come back to me. By the grace, I am able to speak out what would bring good to all."
> "I consider action greater than dependence on fate. He who depends on fate confounds himself."
> "There is no sight equal to learning, no austerity equal to

truthfulness, no misery like passion, and no happiness equal to following the ideal of renunciation."

"The secret meaning of the Vedas is truth; of truth, self-control; of self-control, freedom from all limitations. This is the substance of all scriptures."

"Purity of conduct is the greatest purity. To think of God continuously, to worship Him, to chant His name and sing His praises- this is the best way of attaining the highest good."

The importance of the *Mahabharata* had been accepted by all. The *Bhagavad Gita* which is a part of it is the most popular and significant work of perennial importance. We shall study the philosophy of the *Gita* elsewhere in this book. In the meanwhile, Ananda-vardhana's words about the *Mahabharata* may be quoted here: "The *Mahabharata* teaches man ultimately to renounce the vanity of earthly glories and attain *dharma* (righteousness), *vairagya* (renunciation), *shanti* (peace) and *moksha* (salvation). Vyasa himself remarks in this epic that he has sung the glory of the Lord and that his epic is the Narayana Katha (The story of the Lord), thus clearly indicating what the message of his epic is; for the story of the Pandavas is only an occasion, the purpose being to reveal the greatness of the Lord. Therefore, one should shun all the worldliness and love the Lord."

The Story of Ramayana

The *Ramayana* occupies a very important position in Indian culture. Valmiki is the traditional author of the *Ramayana*. The story of this epic too is well known. Yet, for those who are not acquainted with it, a summary of the story is being given here.

Dasharatha was the beloved ruler of the kingdom of Ayodhya. He had three queens, Kaushalya, Kaikeyi and Sumitra. But the king was childless. Hence, yearning for sons, he performed a sacrifice to which he invited all the great sages, with Vashishtha as their head. The sacrifice was successful. From the sacred fire on the altar there arose a celestial being of matchless beauty, holding in his arms a certain edible thing which when eaten causes conception. This was divided among the three queens. In due course of time Queen Kaushalya gave birth to Rama, who was loved by one and all because of his excellent virtues; Kaikeyi gave birth to Bharata, and Sumitra gave birth to two sons named Lakshmana and Shatrughana. All the four brothers were extremely virtuous and had abiding affection for each other. Rama was an ideal brother and therefore he enjoyed the affection of all his brothers. As the princes grew up they received education worthy of princes. When they were 16 years old, Vishvamitra, a great ascetic, came to the court of their father in search of help against ferocious demons, who used to tease the sages and destroy the peace of their hermitage. All the four brothers were ready to go with him, but he chose Rama because he knew the lad's miraculous powers and recognized him as a divine being. Laxmana loved Rama too much. Hence Rama along with his brother Laxmana followed Vishvamitra, fought the demons and destroyed them.

Vishvamitra, then, brought Rama and Lakshmana to the kingdom of Mithila to attend the sacrificial rite performed by King Janaka in order to find a suitable match for his foster daughter of great talent and beauty, Sita. King Janaka addressed the sage in these words: "O best of ascetics, this is the famous effulgent bow. Whosoever succeeds in stringing it, shall get the hand of my daughter." Many princes tried their luck, but they could not string the bow. Thereupon Rama took the mighty bow, and having fixed its string, bent it easily and gracefully, and even broke it into two pieces. Thus Rama won and wedded Sita.

When Rama came back to Ayodhya, his father Dasharatha decided that the time had come when he should give up his power and install Rama as prince regent. With the consent of his subjects, therefore, he arranged that Rama should the next day be anointed ruler. The whole kingdom rejoiced because their beloved Rama was to be installed as ruler. But a wicked maid servant of Kaikeyi did not like it. She was in the service of Kaikeyi. The name of the maid servant was Manthara. Manthara aroused a furious jealousy for Rama in the heart of Kaikeyi and advised her to take advantage of two boons granted by the King to her at one time. Those boons had to be granted because Dasharatha could not break his word. Manthara advised Kaikeyi to ask the King to place Bharata on the throne and to exile Rama for 14 years.

Kaikeyi was under the evil influence of Manthara. She asked the King to grant these boons. When she insisted on the fulfilment of his promises, the king was overwhelmed, but when Rama came to know about all this, he gladly offered to renounce the throne and go into exile for 14 years. Shortly afterwards, he left Ayodhya accompanied by his loving wife Sita and devoted brother Lakshmana. When Rama took leave of his mother Kaushalya, she said to him : "May the law of truth and righteousness, to which you adhere so strictly, protect you always."

When Rama initially begged Sita not to follow him, she had replied: "Wherever Rama goes, there goes Sita. O Rama, if I have your love, sufferings and hardships of a forest life shall become experiences of joy. Where you are, it is heaven, and where you are not, everything is darkness." And Rama had also then said, "Even heaven will not be heaven to me without you by my side."

Immediately after Rama's departure, King Dasharatha, whose very life and soul Rama had been, suddenly passed away. He was unable to bear separation from Rama. Bharata was not in Ayodhya when all this happened. He had gone to the place of his maternal uncle. When he returned to Ayodhya he came to know all this. He blamed his mother, wept for his father and decided to search out Rama and give him the throne. So he went to the forest, searched out Rama and requested him to accept the throne that rightly belonged to him. But Rama told him that the father's word had to be honoured and hence he could not accept the request. Thereupon Bharata had to go back to Ayodhya at the behest of Rama, but he carried the sandles of Rama and kept them on the throne and ruled the kingdom as Rama's regent.

Rama continued his journey in the forest. He went southward along the bank of the river Godavari and lived a forester's life. One day when Sita was alone in her cottage, Ravana, the king of Lanka, appeared in the disguise of a beggar and stealthily abducted her. He entreated Sita to become his queen, but Sita was an embodiment of chastity and purity and was solely devoted to her husband Rama. She refused even to look at Ravana. Therefore Ravana who was the demon king and had conquered gods and men, in fact the whole world, took away Sita to his Lanka and imprisoned and tortured her to force her to accept his will. But Sita remained adamant.

When Rama and Lakshmana returned to their cottage they did not find Sita. Their grief was boundless at the missing of Sita. They set out in her search and met a dying bird Jatayu who told them that Ravana had taken away Sita forcibly to his Lanka. Rama and Lakshmana then set out in search of Lanka. On their way they met a mighty race of monkeys. In the Ramayana monkeys and demons are imaginative transformations of the aboriginal tribes. Hanumana, the monkey warrior, met Rama and Lakshmana first of all and they were taken to Sugriva, the exiled King of monkeys. Sugriva sought the help of Rama in regaining his lost kingdom from his elder brother Bali. Rama helped him in regaining his lost kingdom. Sugriva then promised Rama to help him in searching Sita. Hanumana and his associates at last found the unknown Lanka of Ravana and informed Rama about Sita and Lanka.

Rama and his associates like Sugriva and Hanumana decided to attack Lanka to free Sita from the imprisonment of Ravana. Lanka was situated away from the mainland of India in an island surrounded by sea. A bridge was built by the monkeys connecting the southernmost point of the mainland of India with Lanka – a little squirrel, according to legend, helping in the work. Rama told to the squirrel, "Blessed are you, because you act to the best of your ability." Then he gently stroked the back of the squirrel, as a result of which squirrels to this day bear the marks of Rama's fingers.

When the bridge was complete, Rama and his army entered Lanka and fought a fierce battle with Ravana. After several months' warfare Ravana was killed and conquered. His throne was given to Vibhishana, his younger brother, by Rama, because Vibhishana was devoted to Rama and righteousness. Sita was thus rescued. But Sita had to undergo another ordeal. Some people murmured, "How do we know that Sita is pure after her being in the imprisonment of Ravana." Rama never suspected the chastity of Sita, but in order to dispel the suspicion, Sita undertook the ordeal of fire test. She plunged herself into sacrificial fire. No sooner did this happen than from the flames emerged the god of fire, bearing on his head a throne, and then seated upon the throne he testified that Sita was absolutely pure and chaste. Thus Sita's chastity was established beyond any doubt.

At the expiration of the term of exile, Rama returned to Ayodhya. People of Ayodhya were very much pleased to see Rama, Sita and Lakshmana back in their city. Rama was crowned as the king of Ayodhya and people celebrated this crowning with abundant joy. Rama and Sita lived a King and Queen for many years. But as the luck would have it, some mischievous persons started the whisper that Sita was taken away by a demon like Ravana and had her imprisoned there. Her chastity was thus questioned. The ordeal that Sita had gone through in Lanka was forgotten. The whisper stated that Sita must submit to a further test, or king Rama must forsake her.

Rama was quite sure about Sita's chastity, but being the king, he thought that his conduct should be beyond any suspicion. Therefore, though it was like tearing off his own heart to do it, he very reluctantly banished his Sita to silence the whisper. Sita was left in a forest where sage Valmiki lived. He took Sita in his hermitage. At that time she was pregnant. In course of time, she gave birth to two sons (twins), Lava and Kusha. Both the sons lived without knowing that Rama was their father. Inspired by Sita's story, Valmiki composed his classic epic Ramayana and taught Lava and Kusha to sing its story. In Ayodhya, Rama was advised to perform *Ashvamedha Yajna*, which needed his wife as per its rite. Rama's people requested him to remarry, but he refused to do so. He said, "This is impossible. My life is Sita's." Under the circumstances, a golden statue of Sita was prepared to enable Rama to complete his sacrifice. Just at that time Valmiki together with Lava and Kusha came to the place.

At the bidding of the sage, the two brothers sang the story of Ramayana in the presence of Rama and a vast audience of his subjects. When they came to tell of Sita's exile, Rama's grief was beyond control. Beholding his grief, Valmiki said: "Do not grieve. I will bring Sita here." Then, to the unspeakable joy of Rama, Sita, his wife, appeared on the stage. But suddenly from the assembled multitude, even at that moment, there arose a murmur; "The test. The test." Hearing this, Sita appealed to the gods to exonerate her. In reply, the earth instantly opened at her feet; and crying out "Here is the test" she disappeared into the bosom of her mother because she was born of earth, her very name meaning "furrow". At this, naturally enough, Rama's sorrow was overwhelming and people lamented loudly. But Sita had disappeared.

Presently a messenger from the gods appeared and announced that Rama's mission, which was to bring peace and happiness to all the world, was fulfilled. Thereupon Rama, realizing to the full his true Self, departed out of his bodily shell and joined his beloved Queen Sita in his celestial abode.

To the non-Indians the *Ramayana* may look like an imaginary epic story. But the wise Indians see both in the *Ramayana* and the *Mahabharata* deeper meanings than the apparent trappings.

The *Mahabharata* is actually an account of the war between the good and evil tendencies going on in the heart of every sensible man. The Pandavas signify good tendencies, while the Kauravas stand for the evil ones. Krishna stands for discretion or wisdom. Thus the *Mahabharata* is a poetic and symbolic account of the battle between spiritual and material urges of man.

In the same way, the *Ramayana* has its inner import. Rama is the *Brahman* and Sita *Prakriti*. Rama may be thought to be the spiritual tendency and Sita may be considered to be the inner peace of mind. Ravana may be considered to be the material tendency that tries to molest the peace.

Even if one is not going to grasp the inner meanings of the epics like the *Ramayana* and the *Mahabharata*, one should be able to understand at least this much that both these great works try to underline the fact that God is Truth. Rama is prepared to respect the words of his father even though the circumstances were such that he could have avoided the exile very easily. But Rama stands for Truth for God is Truth. That is why Rama is not considered to be any ordinary prince. He was God, a divine incarnation. Ravana stood for falsehood. He challenged the might of Truth present in the form of Rama and was destroyed.

In the *Mahabharata* the Pandavas stood for Truth and, therefore, Krishna who was a divine incarnation supported them. The Kauravas stood for untruth. Even though they appeared to be very strong and organized (Kauravas had the most trustworthy warriors on their side like Bhishma, Karna, Dronacharya, etc.) they were defeated. "Dharma eva jayate" (Truth alone conquers), never falsehood. These epics thus inspire people to move on the path of Truth despite obstacles and ordeals because Truth alone conquers ultimately.

Life from the Vedic Period to the Epic Age

It will be worthwhile to have a glimpse of life that the Indians led at that time.

The Western people have generally believe that Indians are other-worldly. But if we look to the Vedas, this misconception proves to be unfounded. For example, we find that the urge for material comforts is present in the hymns of all the Vedas. The *Rig Veda* says, "O Soma, give us light, give us heaven, give us all good fortune." "Soma gives cows, Soma gives swift horses, Soma gives brave, clever sons, skilful in household work, desirous of performing sacrifices and magnifying the glory of their father." The *Atharva Veda* tells us , "This world is most dear to us." The Vedic seer prays, "I am weaving the song of life. Please do not break the yarn of life." "May we live for one hundred years with sound eyes, ears, arms and mind." The Aitareya Brahmana tells us, "Indra helps only those persons who are active." The seers stressed the unity in society, because obstacles can be won only through the combined efforts. "The river containing stones and dirt is flowing. Friends, walk together, walk straight and cross this river." (RV X.53.8)

I may give some statements from the Vedas to prove the point:

> "Give us great wealth for our sons. Give us great wealth for our grandsons. Give us great wealth for our habitations."
> "O Varuna, may I not have to speak of the poverty of any dear relative to any rich people. May I not be wanting in the necessary wealth." "O king Varuna, may I not have to live upon the earnings of others. "Man should care for wealth and should try to get it through rightful means."

Family life was marked by satisfaction. At the time of marriage the bridegroom would say to his bride, "You are song, I am its Sweetness; you are earth, I am heaven. I take your hand in my hand so that you may live with your husband till old age."

At the time of *Saptapadi*, a ceremony of marriage, the bridegroom says, "May not our friendship break at any time. Let us together pledge to lead life together with happiness and may we try to come to a harmonious viewpoint." Wife was considered equal to her husband.

Every religious rite required the presence of both husband and wife, The *Atharva Veda* states, "You both enjoy prosperity and good luck by following the eternal laws and truthfulness." A woman was actually the queen of her house after marriage. The *Atharva Veda* declares, "You become a queen after reaching your husband's house." The *Rig Veda* declares, "In fact wife is home." (RV III.53.4) One hymn states, "O noble-hearted Indra, bestow good sons and prosperity on this lady. Give her ten sons and make her husband the eleventh son." (RV X.85) What was meant through this statement was the fact that the husband should be given that affection which is usually given to the last child. In the Vedic period, wives used to follow their husbands even to forests.

Indeed in the Vedic period family life was full of sweetness and harmony. One seer gives his blessings in the following words:

> "I shall unite your hearts, unite your minds and make you free from rancour. May son be obedient to father and mother. May the wife always speak with husband in sweet words. May brother not bear hatred for his brother, and may a sister love her sister. May all be of one mind and have high ideas and talk sweetly. May your food and water be one, i.e. may you share your water and food with each other. . . . May everyone express good wishes at night and at dawn." (*Atharva Veda* III.30, 1-3, 6-7)

It was considered that a person cannot become a responsible member of society unless he becomes a father. A person devoid of a son cannot attain heavenly happiness (*Aitareya Brahmana* VII, 15). The most important thing in education was character. This is illustrated in a story. Once the goddess of learning approached a teacher and told him, "Please keep me. I am your treasure. Please do not give me to any person who is full of envy and dissatisfaction and is not straightforward in his dealing or whose desires are uncontrolled. Please hand me over to such a person who is pure, attentive, intelligent and of good conduct." (*Samhitopanishad-Brahman*, Chap. III)

A pupil used to reside in the house of his teacher and remain as a member of that family. Thus a synthesis between knowledge and action was aimed at. He used to imbibe the good characteristics of his teacher. We have the example of Aruni who tried to stop the flow of water but failing in doing so himself filled the crack through his body.

The subjects taught were comprehensive, e.g. religion, literary knowledge, grammar, astronomy, medicine, etc. The method of teaching was dialogue, or question-answer. The pupil would ask a question and the teacher would enlighten him. Literacy was given top priority. It is evident from the claim of King Ashvapati Kaikeya, "There is no illiterate person in my kingdom" (*Chhandogya Upanishad* V.II.5). The noble type of education that was given to the students is evident from the convocation address that used to be given. It used to stress the importance of good character and conduct. (*Taittiriya Upanishad* I, II)

A person was expected to discharge at least four types of obligations – obligation towards gods, obligation towards sages, obligation towards ancestors and obligation towards men. Obligation towards gods was said to be discharged by following religious rites and performing one's duties. Obligation towards sages was discharged through cultivation of knowledge and spreading it, obligation towards the ancestors was discharged through giving birth to progeny, and obligation towards man was discharged through acts of cooperation and nobility (*Shatpatha Brahmana*, 1.7. 2:1-12). Before taking meals symbolically food used to be offered to all types of beings. Thus there flourished a society which was totally free from every type of exploitation and was full of helping hands for the needy persons who could not earn sufficient money due to ill luck

Ideal political societies flourished at that period. There used to be free discussions in the assemblies. The *Rig Veda* gives a description of a person who was victorious in a political assembly. "All friends are pleased with a person who comes home after getting victory in the assembly." (RV X.71.10) Differences of opinion are always there. But after due discussion, we should be able to come to one decision acceptable to one and all. Our aims should be similar, our hearts should be united. There should be a perfect unity. (RV X.191.2-4)

The caste system was totally absent at that time. People followed different professions of their individual choice. The *Purusha Sukta* of the *Rig Veda* tells us that all people of human society are inter-related organically – *Brahmins, Kshatriyas, Vaishyas* and *Shudras* – they are all equally important. There is no question of superiority of any caste. (RV X.90.12)

The Vedas were meant for all. One sage declares in the Yajur Veda, "I am giving my blessings to all – *Brahmins, Kshatriyas, Shudras, Vaishyas*, my own relatives and even people belonging to other nations and societies." (Shukla YV 26.2)

A feeling for universal peace, amity and harmony was prevalent in that ancient society." May all people see me with friendliness; may I look to all with friendly feelings." (YV XXXVI.18) Peace was wished even for the sky, for the earth, for water, for everything.

The picture of the Vedic society that finally emerges before us is very sublime and simple. People loved life, society, truthfulness and mutual cooperation. What is significant is the fact that they could think about the highest truth even at that time. We shall study this point at the appropriate place. Suffice it to say here that Hindu customs that are prevalent even at present are to an extent derived from the Vedic period. However, it must be added that good customs of the Vedic period have been deformed to a great extent, as is evident from the caste system as prevalent in Hindu society at present.

Ramayana and Mahabharata Period

It is clear from the pages of the *Ramayana* that the Indian society of that period had respect for the basic values of life. Rama was such an ideal king that he made great sacrifices to preserve peace and harmony in society. He sacrificed kingdom and even his wife for placing right ideals before society. Valmiki has rightly stated that Rama is virtue incarnate *(Ramah vigrahavan dharmo)*.

It appears that ascetic ideals were given utmost importance. It was the duty of a king to protect virtuous persons from the attack of the demonic persons. Casteism was not prevalent, because even though Vishvamitra was a Kshatriya, he indulged in the acts of penance, associated with Brahmins, and Parashurama who was a Brahmin, became a great wielder of weapons. Even though the monarchy system of government was in vogue, kings respected the wishes of the subjects. They were brave and dutiful. They did not stick to power and used to give up their thrones to their eldest son in old age and retire for spiritual advancement. Love and affection prevailed in the families.

However, there were some persons who liked to lead a very unprincipled life. They were persons of destructive tendencies. Such persons were known as demons (*a-sura*, i.e. unrighteous persons) Spiritual ideals were respected and given due importance. Some persons see in the Ramayana a conflict between the Aryas and non-Aryas. But this is only a fiction. The Aryas did not come form any land out of India. India is a big country. Hence, there is every possibility that people belonging to divergent customs and rites must have flourished in India itself.

Anyway, it is clear that the *Ramayana* reflects the high type of culture that prevailed in India at that period. The attempt of the author of the *Ramayana* shows that at that time high values ruled the actual conduct of the leading characters of that time. The *Mahabharata* indicates that the harmony in the families that prevailed at the time of the *Ramayana* was losing its hold. The very conflict of the Pandavas and the Kauravas indicates that envy had entered the hearts of people. Hence, family life began to lose its old harmony.

But equally dominant was the element that wanted to hold aloft the flag of purity and moral integrity. Krishna was the leader of this tendency. Righteousness has to be established in society, because in its absence social organization cannot subsist. The *Bhagavadgita*, which is a constituent part of the *Mahabharata*, declares that God will never allow the evil and destructive tendencies to overpower the constructive and good element. Whenever there shall be a big threat to the existence of good, God Himself will incarnate on earth and destroy the evil elements. (BG IV.7) Arjuna wanted to shirk the battle because he was required to wield his weapons against his elders. But Krishna warned him that this could not be done. The destruction of the evil-minded could not be avoided. It was immaterial whether these elements were the relatives of the Pandavas. Arjuna was merely an instrument of the divine plan of the destruction of the evil. (BG XI.33) Even in the absence of Arjuna, this plan would be carried out because the evil elements cannot be allowed to play their destructive role. (BG XI.32)

In fact the very purpose of writing the *Mahabharata* was to show that good alone prevails, the evil has to perish. Life is no doubt a conflict between the good and the evil, but this conflict would have to end in the victory of good. This is the will of God. It is not a decree of a mortal human being which can be challenged. And this law of the survival of the good and the weakening of the evil is imprinted on the pages of history.

This message of the *Mahabharata* has left an indelible impression on the mind of an Indian. Mahatma Gandhi's *satyagraha* battle against the mighty British force was prompted by it. The *Mahabharata* shows that at that time people had a firm faith in the ultimate victory of dharma and the people who believed in the ultimate victory of dharma and the people who believed in the supremacy of dharma fought fierce battles against the evil and never succumbed to the might of the evil. Prosperity can come to society, only if dharma is given due importance. Vyasa states, "Material prosperity and satisfaction of rightful desires can be possible only if dharma is maintained. It is amazing that despite this fact, people try to go against the dictates of dharma." *(dharmat arthashcha kamashcha, sa dharmah kim na sevyate).*

The Puranas

The Puranas have played a very important role in preserving and propagating the ideals of Indian culture. The method of the Puranas is based on a study of human nature. Most of people are not inclined towards serious studies. The very fact that in India very few persons are really acquainted with the details of the Upanishads, but are acquainted with the Puranic stories indicates that the Puranas are more popular than even the Vedas. The reason of this popularity is simple. The Puranas try to present the message in the garb of stories. Most of people find these stories very interesting, and a few can go deep and find out the message contained in them.

The Puranas are history if we take the term history in a broad sense. One of the characteristics of the Puranas is "vamshacharita", or the lives of dynasties, the Solar and Lunar in particular. This vamshacharita has helped modern historians in the act of reconstructing our past. For example, the historical dynasties of the Shishunagas, Nandas, Mauryas, Shungas, Andhras and Guptas are actually mentioned in them. The facts given in the *Vishnu Purana* about the Maurya dynasty (386-185 B.C.) have proved to be quite reliable, as has been admitted by Vincent Smith. In the same way, the *Matsya Purana* gives a real picture of the Andhra dynasty, and the *Vayu Purana* of the rule of Chandragupta I of the Gupta period.

According to the traditional view, there are 18 major Puranas and 18 or 20 minor Puranas. The names of the major Puranas along with the number of shlokas are mentioned below:

Sl.No.	*Names*	*No. of Shlokas*
1.	Brahma	10,000
2.	Padma	55,000
3.	Vishnu	23,000
4.	Vayu	24,000
5.	Bhagavata	18,000
6.	Narada	25,000
7.	Markandeya	9,000
8.	Agni	10,500
9.	Bhavishya	14,500
10.	Brahmavaivarta	18,000
11.	Linga	11,000
12.	Varaha	24,000
13.	Skanda	81,000
14.	Vamana	10,000
15.	Kurma	17,000
16.	Matsya	14,000
17.	Garuda	19,000
18.	Brahmanda	12,000

It is worth noting that the Puranas begin with the Brahma and end with the Brahmanda in between being the Brahmavaivarta. It connotes that the Puranas deal with the creation lore which gives us the knowledge beginning with the Brahma or the Creator and ending with the Brahmanda or the creation. Thus we are reminded of the Brahma in the beginning, in the middle and at the end. That is why a famous statement about the Puranas is in vogue that herein Hari (God) is sung of in the beginning, middle and end, i.e. everywhere.

Some read Shiva in the place of Vayu and Devi-Bhagavata instead of the Bhagavata. In order to accommodate these divergent views, Pargiter takes their number to be 19 by including both Siva and Vayu.

The *Mahapuranas* have been divided by the *Padmapurana* into

Sattvika, Rajas and *Tamasa.* Vishnu, Narada, Bhagavata, Garuda, Padma and Varaha are *Sattvika*; Brahmanda, Brahmavaivarta, Brahma, Vamana and Bhavishya are *Rajas*; Matsya, Kurma, Linga, Shiva, Agni and Skanda are *Tamasa.*

However on the the basis of the names of the deities referred in respective Puranas, they can be classified in the following way too:

1.	Brahma	*Brahma* and *Padma Puranas*
2.	Surya	*Brahmavaivarta Purana*
3.	Agni	*Agni Purana*
4.	Shiva	*Shiva, Skanda, Linga, Kurma, Vamana, Varaha, Bhavishya, Matsya, Markandeya* and *Brahmanda Puranas*
5.	Vishnu	*Narada, Bhagavata, Garuda* and *Vishnu Puranas*

It should be remembered that the Puranas were written to explain and elucidate the high philosophy and religion of the Vedas and the Upanishads to the common public in an easy and comprehensible language and style. The Vedas are supposed to be "aptavakyas" or the words of authority, i.e. they are to be accepted with faith. The Puranas are the "suhridvakyas" or the advices of friends, i.e. they teach the message of the Vedas in a friendly manner by means of so many events, parables, stories, etc. They are actually the Vedas of the laity. They have given a universality of outlook to their readers. Indian culture and civilization were saved from total disintegration and devastation mainly due to the influence of the Puranas. Not only this, they gave new hope and solace to those who belonged to the oppressed strata of Indian community, and who were kept away from God on the imaginary grounds of caste, sex or any other distinction.

It is unfortunate that the basic aim of the Puranas was forgotten by the half-literate persons who took the responsibility of reciting the Puranas before the common people. The symbolic language of the Puranas was not understood by them and they misinterpreted them either through their own ignorance or mischievousness.

Whether one is a poet or a religious man or a philosopher, one has to convey the high ideas in a symbolic manner. The tradition states that Veda Vyasa was also the author of the Puranas. This statement conveys the fact that the stories of the Puranas must be understood by going to the bottom of the statements or stories because Vyasa was the greatest poet-philosopher-religious soul.

The Symbolism

Vyasa has forced his readers to understand his symbolism. The deities like Ganesha provide a vivid instance of this fact. The Vedantic truth is that the Brahman is the sole truth. This truth, however, cannot be grasped by an ordinary person. It requires an intelligent mind to comprehend it. Ganesha has been represented as having a big head. This big head is the symbol of big capacity of grasping the truth. This truth, however, can be grasped only after listening attentively to the teachings of the great teachers. Ganesha has been represented as having big ears, suggesting his capacity to attentive listening. The teeth of Ganesha suggest his faculty of discretion, two tusks suggest two factors of consideration – good and evil. Ganesha is shown with one of his tusks broken. This implies that only the sole truth that the Brahman alone is the Real has been attained. Ganesha is considered to be the son of Lord Shiva. This implies that a person who is able to grasp the truth becomes Shiva, a great benefactor of society because there is no selfish tinge in him.

Every Purana is rich in symbols. Only persons of low intelligence take the unusual stories narrated in the Puranas in their literal sense. A person of subtle understanding and spiritual outlook goes beyond the simple story to understand the real meaning. All the gods of Hindu religion are essentially one because the symbols imply this very fact.

The name Krishna is derived from the root *krish* (kṛṣ) which means to draw or to attract. Thus Krishna is that innermost Being of our heart that attracts us. According to another interpretation, one who is the supreme Godhead, who is the biggest and who is spread all over is known as Krishna. Rama and Krishna both have blue-coloured bodies. Blue colour represents infinity. Hence, both Rama and Krishna are the forms or incarnations of the Supreme Reality. Some persons think that the divine character of Rama is not deducible from incidents like the killing of Bali from a hidden place. They argue Rama should have fought Bali face to face.

In reply to such a criticism, it can be stated that every spiritual story contains some inner meaning. The Bali story too has a deep meaning.

Bali was the strong but vicious brother of Sugriva. He represents lust or the lower nature of man. Sugriva represents the higher virtues of man. Bali had a boon that whosoever came before him to fight shall lose half his strength and this half strength shall go to Bali. The implication is that if an object of lust is before an individual, the latter is weakened and the fire of lust becomes invincible. Hence, it is essential for spiritual progress, at least initially, to avoid the presence of such persons and objects as may excite one's lust. To prove this very point, Rama was shown as killing Bali from behind the trees. While reading the Puranas, one should never forget that they are spiritual works. To put any gross physical interpretation on them is not at all justified. To understand the real meaning of the Puranas, one has to have a higher, spiritual attitude to life.

As has been stated earlier, the persons who took up the responsibility of reciting the Puranas lacked the necessary intelligence and spiritual height. Therefore, they failed to correctly interpret and explain the real spiritual message of the Puranas, they even misinterpreted them. For example, the very first *shloka* of the *Bhagavata Purana* explicitly states that the Brahman alone is real. Everything else has phenomenal existence. It has also been stated that one single non-dual reality has been given different names by wise persons (Bh. Pu. I-2-11). Even in the last chapter, it has been expressly stated that the Supreme Reality alone has been the object of narration in the Purana (Bh. Pu. 12-13-19). The Real has been given the name of Krishna *(Krishnastu bhagavana swayam).*

To understand the real meaning of the Purana, in fact every Purana, one needs a spiritual attitude. The *Bhagavata* has been described as the meditational language *(samadhi bhasha)* of Vyasa. Puranic lore has been considered to be the foremost learning *(Puranam sarvashastranam pratham brahmana smritam).* The Puranas are devoted to God and have inspired devotion in every reader. They have taught the lesson of morality *(achara-hinam na punanti vedah).* They are moreover encyclopaedian in character. The *Agni Purana* can be considered to be the first encyclopaedia of the world *(agneye hi purane'smin sarva-vidyah pradarshitah).*

We can distinguish between the Hindu, the Jaina and the Bauddha Puranas, but they follow the same pattern. All these Puranas helped readers to understand the Vedic teachings, as Vedas are the store-houses of many kinds of thought. The importance of the Puranas can be understood from the fact that they are considered to be the fifth Veda. Nobody can understand the real import of Indian culture without a proper study of the Puranas.

For example, the Puranas present the concept of four *Yugas.* These are: *Sat Yuga, Treta Yuga, Dwapara Yuga* and *Kali Yuga. Sat Yuga* is marked by the truthfulness and simplicity of people, *Treta Yuga* is marked by 25 per cent diminution in the ideal of truthfulness, *Dwapara Yuga* is marked by 50 per cent diminution in that ideal, and *Kali Yuga* is marked by 75 per cent diminution in that ideal of truthfulness. Thus the four *Yugas* have their own features.

At present we are living in the *Kali Yuga.* According to the Vishnu *Purana,* in this age the rights of people shall remain obscure and confused; no property shall remain secure, and no joy shall be lasting. The *Bhagavata Purana* gives a detailed description of the characteristic features of life in the *Kali Yuga* (12-2). Exploitation of people, absence of higher values of life, addiction to sexual acts, drought, hypocricy in religious life and such other undesirable things shall become common in the *Kali Yuga.*

The Puranas teach that man is responsible for every act done by him. He will have to reap the fruits of what he sows. There is no escape. Fate is actually the result of one's past acts. Man can build his future by doing good acts and by patiently bearing the consequences of his past life.

Body is an instrument of action. Human body is not to be decried, because the ultimate object of life, the realization of the intrinsic worth and nature of immortal soul, can be gained only through human body, which can be attained by a man only after having suffered in many non-human forms. The Puranas generally glorify the house hold life *(grihasthashrama).* Any person who thinks about entering *Sanyasa* without first leading a married life has to be condemned, because, he acts against human nature and the spirit of religion. The Puranas present the Brahman of the Upanishads in the form of a personal god. Religious aspirations can be fulfilled only through devotion to a personal deity. Devotion demands that there must be a god who responds whenever a worshipper invokes his aid. Such a god should not only be helpful, but be an abode of beauty, bravery, bountifulness, capacity to do anything, and unmatched strength. The Puranas, therefore, present this very kind of god in Krishna, Shiva, Ganesha, Kali, etc. One should not think that as the Puranas contain references to more than one god they believed in the existence of many gods. The Bhagavata tells us that persons give names of their liking to God. God is one, but He is addressed by many names depending upon the liking of the persons. The henotheism of the *Rig Veda* is present in the Puranas too. The *Bhagavata* (1-1-3) calls itself a fruit fallen from the tree of the Vedas.

The Puranas hold devotion to be the highest ideal of man. God can be realized only through devotion. They are fools who think that God can be realized through ritualism or even through the pathway of knowledge. The beauty of devotion is that it has no place for distinction of any type. Literate, illiterate, man, woman, even animals can reach God if they love Him. For devotion neither scriptural knowledge is needed nor is the noble birth or any other thing of the type necessary. The Puranas in this way brought equality in society and destroyed social distance.

The theory of incarnation became popular because of the Puranas. Apart from satisfying the feelings and cravings of a devoted heart, this theory brings courage and confidence in the hearts of people even in the darkest hours. Indians had to feel the brunt of many attacks, but Indian culture remained alive with enthusiasm and energy only because of the theory of incarnation. People believed as taught by the Puranas that the oppressor shall be destroyed in the course of time by God. Whenever there is an aggression of the evil over the good and it appears that the good shall be eliminated, God takes incarnation and gives a crushing defeat to the evil.

Devotion has its social aspect too. A real devotee is not only interested in the worship of God, he is also very sensitive to the sufferings of people all around him. Prahalada, a paragon of devotees, declares that he is not interested in seeking his individual salvation. He wants that all people should get liberation first and would like to be the last to get it. Tulasidasa, himself a great devotee and thinker, states that the heart of a saint is like butter which melts at the fire of the suffering of his fellow beings.

One should not think that the Puranas are merely religious works. Some of them can be termed to be the specimen of the best poetry. For example, the description of nature found in the Bhagavata Purana is very charming and suggestive. The *Bhagavata* is considered to be the literary incarnation of God *(vangamayavatara)*. There cannot be a better tribute to the literary qualities of any work. And it is no vain description. The excellent literary qualities of the *Bhagavata* are evident to any reader who takes the trouble of perusing it.

The devotional teaching of the Puranas inspired art and literature to scale new heights. Subjects like *Vastu-shastra* (art of building dwellings), *sthapatya-kala* (sculpture), *shilpa-shastra, chitra-shastra* (painting), *pratima-shastra* (art of idol making), etc., have been efficiently described in the Puranas. The saint-period of Hindi literature that saw the emergence of gifted poets like Tulasidasa, Suradasa, Nandadasa and a host of others got inspiration from the Purana literature. The *Vishnu Purana* states that poetry, music and literature are the different aspects of God alone (I.22.84). The *Agni Purana* is a storehouse of worldly and spiritual lore (319, 1-11).

While the importance of the Puranas from the standpoint of religion, philosophy, literature, history and culture is beyond any dispute, it has to be admitted that the true import of the Puranas could not be grasped by the general public because of the inapt and inefficient handling of the Puranas by the preachers and reciters. An element of blind faith became dominant and the spiritual kernel was forgotten.

On the whole, however, the Puranas have rendered a good service to Indian culture.

Whether one likes the Puranas or dislikes them, one has to accept that they have influenced the minds of people to a great extent. The rites and rituals, stories, festivals, idol worship and philosophical speculation that are prevalent in Hindu society speak eloquently about the profuse influence of the Puranas on the minds of people. It should not be forgotten that the Jaina and the Buddha religions too are the varieties of the Vedic religion which is supposed to be Sanatana, i.e. eternal. Indian culture is a vast edifice having a place for a lot of varieties.

Smriti Literature

Smritis also occupy a significant place in the domain of Indian culture. They embody the laws formulated by law-givers like Manu, Yajnavalkya, Narada, etc. They can be termed *Dharma-shastras* because they describe the rights and duties of the people and the king. A detailed study of the *smriti* literature is not intended here. But it has to be stated explicitly that Hindu society has been governed by these rules of conduct from ancient times and it is still ruled by these rules. They are more than 100 in number. This does not mean that the *Smritis* have nothing to do with the Vedas. The fact is that they declare themselves to be subservient to the Vedas. The rules suggested by the Smritis have religious sanction. Hence, they are respected by a bulk of Hindu society. The most important Smriti is the Manu-Smriti.

The *Manu Smriti* is a large work. It lays down rules for the students, house-holder, marriage, daily rites, funeral offerings, lawful and forbidden food, impurity and purification, rules regarding women, rules regarding the hermit and ascetic, duties of a king, civil and criminal law, rules for sacrifice and penances, duties of the Brahmins, Kshatriyas, Vaishyas and Shudras. But the basic philosophy of the Vedas is never forgotten. For example, we may note the following statement of the *Smriti:* "Alone man is born, alone he dies, alone he reaps the fruit of good and evil done by him. Laying down on the ground the body of the dead as if it were a clod or a log, the kin depart with face averted; righteousness alone is his companion." Although to enter married life is obligatory, it has been declared that the ultimate spiritual aim of liberation is not to be forgotten by a person. Manu states:

> "When he (a person) sees wrinkles on his face and gray in his hair, a son born to his son, then should the householder fare to the forest."

Statements from some other *Smritis* too may be noted here so that a fair idea about the nature of the *Smritis* may be formed: "Truth is the one mode of winning purity, truth the ship that bears men to heaven, truth weighed against a thousand-horse sacrifices outweighs them, truth is the highest oblation, the highest asceticism, the highest morality, truth is the summit of bliss, by telling truth man attains by himself the highest self which is itself truth." *(Narada Smriti)*

"Truth, honesty, mildness, modesty, purity, wisdom, firmness, self-control, the restraint of the senses, learning, these make up the whole of righteousness." *(Yajnavalkya Smriti)*

"In the midst of that circle abides the self as if a motionless light; it must be known, and knowing it no man is born again to life." *(Yaj. Sm.)*

There are several *smritis*. One list mentions 152. But Manu, Narada, Parashara, Yajnavalkya and a few more are more important than other minor *Smritis*.

In this context, the following words of A.B. Keith are worth noting: "Yajnavalkya formed the subject of a very large number of important commentaries; the best known, the *Mitakshara of Vijnaneshvara*, was written in the south in the 11th century, and constitutes an important treatise on law, which won acceptance in the Deccan and also in Benares and north India; Colebrooke's version of the section on inheritance gave it currency in the English courts in India. The author used the work of *Vishvarupa*, Apararka wrote on the *Smriti* in the 12th century, while Balambhatta Vaidyanatha and his wife Lakshmidevi commented on the *Mitakshara* in an interesting manner, emphasizing the claims of women to property rights."[1]

Thus we find that Indian culture is constituted by the influence of the Vedic literature, the epics like the *Ramayana*, and the *Mahabharata*, the *Puranas* and the *Smritis*. All these works may seem to be separate and different and divergent to a lay man, but in fact one master thought runs in their veins.

NOTE

1. *A History of Sanskrit Literature*, p.447.

3

LITERATURE AND ART

LITERATURE AND art are the vehicles of culture in every society. The term "literature" is very wide. Usually it is supposed to consist of written words. If we take the term in this wide denotation, even the daily news-papers shall be considered to be literature. If the term literature is taken in this wide sense, we can classify literature in two categories, namely books of the moment and the books of eternity. Newspapers are evidently books of the moment and so are the books of stories and novels. Very few books can be placed in the category of the books of eternity. Only books like the *Ramayana* and the *Mahabharata* can be included in the category of books of eternity. Culture is reflected in the books of eternity alone. Only the books of eternal value can contribute to the development of real culture. The Sanskrit word for literature is "Sahitya" meaning literature that contains an element of social welfare and significance. Thus, etymologically speaking, literature aims at the furtherance of social welfare or spiritual development. The very aim of Indian literature is to help in the destruction of what is hostile to social welfare *(shivetara-kshataye).* We may enumerate a few characteristic features of Indian literature, before we proceed further.

Characteristic Features of Indian Literature

Indian literature has some peculiar features which mark it out from the literature of the West.

The very first feature is its synthetic character. In the domain of religion, we find a synthesis of knowledge, devotion and action; in the domain of social organisation, we find a synthesis in Brahmin, Kshatriya, Vaishya and Shudra *varnas*; in the same strain, we find a spirit of synthesis of happiness and unhappiness, rise and fall, separation and meeting, joy and pain in Indian literature. All these different sentiments are submerged ultimately in the divine bliss.

Indian literature is always optimistic, because sorrow cannot strike the immortal soul. That is why tragedy has no place in ancient Indian dramas. The second noteworthy feature is that Indian literature is inspired by religion. Dharma (religion) in India not only finds its way in the domain of spirituality, it also finds a place in the empirical world, because dharma is that principle which sustains both individual life and social organisation. That is why we find dominance of religious influence in Indian literature. The great works of India were always inspired by religion. For example, the names of the *Ramayana*, the *Mahabharata*, the *Raghuvamsha*, the *Ramacharita Manasa* and the *Padmavata* may be mentioned in this context. The third characteristic of Indian literature is that it gives noteworthy importance to nature. The rivers, mountains, trees are not only beautifully described but even worshipped. Nature has been very bountiful to India. The Himalayas, in the north, the ocean on three sides, the rivers like the Ganges, Godavari, etc., and the beautiful forests have given a rare beauty to India. The literary works of India right from the Vedas to the Puranas and the epics contain enchanting descriptions of nature. The *Ritusamhara* and the *Meghaduta*, well known works of Kalidasa, are remarkable examples of the description of nature and its impact on human heart.

The fourth notable feature is, that in ancient India prose composition was less liked as compared with poetic compositions. Even the works on medicine were composed in poetic forms.

Now, we will proceed further to have a glimpse of major ancient works of India to have a better idea of Indian literature.

The story of Indian literature begins right from the *Rig Veda*, which has been accepted as the oldest work of the world. Sanskrit was the chief language of ancient India, although other languages also flourished. We shall merely give the names of outstanding works here to avoid an increase in the bulk of the present work.

(a) *Poetical Works*

The *Ramayana* of Valmiki and the *Mahabharata* of Vyasa are the most venerable epics of India. We have already given their descriptions in this very book earlier.

(i) Ashvaghosha was a great Buddhist writer. His two major poetic works are *Saundarananda* and *Buddhacharita*. Both the works are concerned with the tale of the great Buddha. Even though religious in concept, the works are pieces of great artistic beauty. For example, let us have a look at the picture of a sleeping beauty of the harem:

> "And one lay resplendent, holding a flute in her hand, while her white garment slipt from her bosom, like unto a river whose banks laugh with the foam of her waves, and in whose lotuses long rows of bee delight."

Here is another illustration:

> "So when the evil one had retired worsted, the sky became calm, the moon shone forth, flowers fell in rain from heaven on the earth; night shone clear like a maiden free from stain."

(ii) Kalidasa is the most famous poet of India. His major works are *Ritusamhara, Meghaduta, Raghuvamsha, Kumara-sambhava, Shakuntala Vikramovashi* and *Malvikagnimitra*. Kalidasa is the master of language and style. His knowledge of human psychology too is superb. Here are some examples from the *Meghaduta*:

> "Or perhaps, placing her lute on her lap, whose dark garment proclaims her grief, she will seek to sing a song wherein she has worked my name, but, scarse able to move the string which her tears have bedewed, she will forget the air which she herself hath made."
> "Wife, counsellor, companion, dearest disciple in every loving art; in taking thee tell me what of me hath not pitiless Death taken."

(iii) Bharavi's *Kiratarjuniya* is also a famous work. He excels in the observation of beauties. Let us take an example:

> "For Love's consecration the lady night raised aloft the moon with its shimmering sea of beams and its spots full in view, like a silver chalice decked with lotuses."

(iv) *Shishupala-vadha* of Magha is another significant epic. Here is an example:

> "As the hosts of the king with unbroken flow, with unceasing clamour in their proud onslaughts, advanced against the vast armies of Krishna, there arose a battle swaying to and fro as when the waters of the streams mingle with the foaming waves of ocean."

There is a great number of poets and poetic works. It is not possible to make a mention of all of them here. But it is proper to mention here that mostly the aims of poets were two: winning of fame and giving pleasure.

There are various types of poetry, secular, religious, didactic, etc.

(b) *The Didactic Fable*

Panchatantra and the *Hitopadesha* are the famous works which try to give instruction through stories.

(c) *Romances*

Dandin's *Dashakumaracharita*, Bana's *Harshacharita* and *Kadambari* can be mentioned in this context. The *Kadambari* is the example of the excellent prose of the Sanskrit.

(d) *Champus*

Champus are a mixture of verse and prose. This form of literature is perhaps peculiar to India alone. *Madalasa Champu, Nala Champu, Jivanadhara Champu, Ramayana Champu* and *Svahasudhakara Champu* may be mentioned here. *Champus* generally contain love stories.

Thus we find that various types of poetic compositions are found in Sanskrit, the ancient India's language of culture. Not only this, a thorough discussion on the theories of poetry was also undertaken. Bhamaha, Vishvanatha, Mammata, Rajashekhara and Rudrata are some of the names that may be mentioned here. Even a Western scholar like Keith writes in praise of the high standard of poets of India:

"Moreover, the Sanskrit poets had command of a language capable of finer sound effects than even Greek at its best. . . . They could successfully manage metres of great complexity but remarkable beauty, and they were conscious experts in the task of matching sound to sense, an art practised indeed by Greek and Roman poets alike, but with far less adequate means and with much less subtlety. Their use of alliteration is often overdone, but they resemble Virgil in their power to make it yield effective results, an art in which his followers and notably Lucan were markedly deficient. Their love for metaphor and simile . . . often they show a richness of fancy and power of happy phraseology which is not paralleled either in Greek or Latin poetry."[1]

(e) *Dramas*

India can boast of having the best types of dramas. The Natya Shastra of Bharata is the oldest and most authoritative work on plays. Some people are of the opinion that the plays came to India from the Greek literature. But this theory is baseless. India has the convention of play from the very beginning of its recorded culture. Bharata has mentioned 10 principal types of plays. Kalidasa and Bhasa are the most famous drama writers of ancient India. *Abhijnana-Shakuntala* the most famous play of Kalidasa, has impressed even the Western scholars due to its novelty and fineness of expression. Shudraka's play *Mrichchhakatika* is another famous play.

Vishakhadatta *(Mudra-rakshasa)*, Harsha *(Ratnavali* and *Nagananda)*, Bhavabhuti *(Uttara-ramacharita)* and Bhattanarayana *(Venisamhara)* are some other well known names in the domain of drama writers. In fact there are a number of dramas in Sanskrit. Thus we find that Indian culture is rich from the standpoint of literature.

India abounds in the writings called *Bhakti stotras* or *Stuti kavya* Philosophy and religion always attracted great Indian minds. They composed panegyrics in praise of gods. Thus the *Ramayana* contains a *Stotra* called *"Aditya-hridaya"*. It was taught by the sage Agastya to Rama. The *Mahabharata* contains *"Vishnu Sahasranama Stotra"*. It was taught by Bhishma to Yudhishthira. The *Markandeya Purana* contains *Durga Stotra*.

Philosophical *Stotras* are very important. Shankara's *Stotras* are quite famous. His compositions bearing the titles *Ananda lahari*, *Govindashtaka, Moha-mugdara*, etc., are very popular. He has preached the gospel of the *Advaita* through these *Stotras*. Jayadeva's *Gita-govinda* too is a very popular writing. It is not possible to give the names of various *Stotras* as they are too many in number.

And before we conclude a discussion about literature, let us inform our readers that Indian literature also contains amorous poems. Bhirtrahari composed three different types of poems called *Shringara Shataka, Niti Shataka* and *Vairagya Shataka*. It will be desirable to give some examples:

"O wandering heart, stray not in the forest of woman's fair body, nor in the steeps which are her breasts, for there lurks love, the highwayman."

"Without parallel, O fair one, assuredly is thy marksmanship. With thy bowstrings, not thine arrows, thou dost pierce our hearts."

"When we see not our beloved one, we are content to long to gaze upon her; seen, our one aim is the joy of close embraces; embraced, our one prayer is that her body and our own may be made one."

Now one instance from the *Vairagya Shataka*

"For a moment man is a boy, for a moment lovesick youth, for a moment bereft of wealth, for a moment in the height of prosperity; then, at life's end with limbs worn out by old age and wrinkles adorning his face, like an actor, he retires behind the curtain of death."

The *Amaru Shataka* is also a famous poetic composition. An instance from this work too may be given here:

"The house parrot overheard at night some dalliance of the young pair and in the morning began to repeat it unduly before their elders; so the young wife in shame stays his speech by putting in his beaks fragment of ruby from here earring, on the pretext of giving him a pomegranate fruit."

Even satirical literature is present in Sanskrit. Kshemendra in his *Darpa-dalana* has written satires on various aspects of human life. He tells *sanyasi* : "What harm has been done to you by your hair? If you really intend to shave off, shave off your evil tendencies. *Sanyasi*'s robe cannot hide your ignoble mind." In his *Kala Vilasa* he has compared an evil-minded *yogi* with the bird that sits by the side of a river with half-closed eyes watching fishes with a view to eating them up. He has written about a doctor, "I salute you for killing persons. Death has no worries because it has given its duties to you." Nilakantha Dikshita in his *Kali-vidambana* has also written beautiful satire. In one of his satires he states that only that person can get public acclaim who breaks pots or tears off his clothes or brays like a donkey. He speaks of a son-in-law as the 10th planet that controls the destiny of a person in society.

Sanskrit is the most scientific language in the world. Its importance has been recognised even by the science of computer which gives it preference over other languages. This scientific character has been given to this language by the grammarians like Panini, Katyayana, Patanjali, Bhartrahari, etc. The most important grammarian is, of course, Panini, whose grammar, *Ashtadhyayi* even now commands respect. Sanskrit is called the language of the gods *(deva-bhasha)* because of its perfect character. This description of the language seems to be perfectly justified.

Art — A Comprehensive Term

If the *Yajnavalkya Smriti* talks about 14 kinds of learning *(vidya)*, the *Kamasutra* of Vatsyayana tells us about 64 types of *kala* (art). The word *kala* has been used in a wide sense. History, drama, song, etc., are included in this list. Even theft has been included in this list. The list of 64 *kalas* differs from author to author. But there is no doubt that Indian culture has a place for a variety of arts. Literature too can be termed an art, because every art is efficiency in the expression of one's feeling in one way or the other.

There are two kinds of art: useful art and fine art. Manufacturing skills of armours, cloth, ornaments, etc., can be called useful arts. Fine arts have been divided into five kinds—sculpture (art of preparing idols), painting, music and poetry.

The main source of inspiration of arts has been religion. Mostly, the fine arts in India indicate a spirit of dedication to the Supreme.

Architecture *(Shilpa-shastra, Vastu-shastra)* was known to the most ancient India. Its story begins from the Indus Valley civilisation. The existence of works like *Sanatkumaravastushastra*, Shrikumara's *Shilparatna* indicates that architecture was quite evolved in the ancient period. The figure of lions in the Ashoka Pillar is so beautiful that it has been adopted as the national emblem. Many temples that are still in existence proclaim that the art of building had attained a high refinement. The Hindu temple was "first a leafy bower, then a red-hut, and afterwards a cell of wood and brick". Monuments of Ellora and Elephanta and the temples of Khujraho are the standing examples of the glory of India in the domain of sculpture and architecture. *Viharas, Stupas, Chaityas* and such other constructions are the specimen of highly evolved architecture and sculpture.

Even the mountains were cut in the forms of temples as is evident from the Kailasa temple of Ellora and the Jaina temple of the Mount Abu.

But architecture was not confined to religious domain alone. It extended to the building of big castles and forts. P.K. Acharya in his work *Dictionary of Hindu Architecture* has mentioned that works like *Kamikagama, Vastu-tatva, vastu-prabandha* and *Shilpa-shastra-sangraha* exist in India. Their description points to the presence of a highly evolved art of building. But the most extensive information in this direction is provided by the work Manasara. This work uses the term architecture in a wide sense. It declares that before constructing any building, attention should be paid to a systematic plan of the development of a village or a city and related subjects like development of gardens, building of a bazar, roads, streets, bridges, wells, etc. The nature of ground, nature of earth, temperature, sunlight, direction of wind and all other factors should be given due consideration. It has been said that those buildings are the best in which the height of a room is twice the size of width. The influence of Indian architecture can be witnessed in the architecture of Sri Lanka, Cambodia and Java.

Image-making

The tradition of image-making too is quite old in India. The earthen images discovered from the ruins of Mohen-jo-daro contain strong resemblance with figures of men and animals. This very art of image-making finds perfection in the Rampurva Bull of the Gupta period. The *Buddha Jataka* stories inspired the artists to prepare different images. The spiritual inspiration of the image-making art finds its acme in the image of Trimurti at Elephanta and the image of Nataraja of South India. Nataraja expresses the cycle of development and death. It expresses the fact that the universe is not static, it contains a rhythm of rise and fall, life and death. They are fools who think that the world never changes and their material possessions shall remain with them for ever.

The image-making is not confined to religious sphere. Secular field also attracts the artists. Wooden nymphs of Mathura, Female chauri-bearer, probably a *Yakshini*, Didarganj, Patna, *Yakshi Chulakoka* at Bharahut, Central India, Woman bathing under waterfall, *Kankali Tila*, Mathura, Mother fondling child, Bhuvaneswar, Woman with mirror, Bhuvaneswar, Huntress in wild dress, Mysore, and hundreds of other images prove this point. The images at the Khujraho temple are too well known to need any detailed information.

It is thus clear that image-making art was highly developed in India.

Paintings

Indian art of painting has a long tradition of about 2,000 years. The finest specimens of painting can be seen on the walls of Ajanta, which inspired the painting even in Afghanistan, Sri Lanka, Tibet, China and Japan. The paintings of Bodhisatva found in the Ajanta tell us a lot about the highly developed art of painting in India. We should not be surprised at this. Vatsyayana in his *Kamasutra* has included paintings in the list of 64 arts. Princes and wealthy persons used to have picture galleries in their houses. Kalidasa in his works has made a reference to the art of painting. The hero of his famous play *Shakuntala*, King Dushyanta, was himself a great painter. When he remembered everything about Shakuntala on being shown the ring he drew or prepared such a fine painting of Shakuntala that even her friend was surprised. The Puranas contain a reference of painters like Chitralekha. Marriages were settled in ancient India on the basis of the paintings of the bride and bridegroom. Yashodhara, in his commentary on the *Kamasutra*, refers to six limbs of a painting — *Rupabheda, Pramana, Bhava, Lavanya-yojana* and *Varnikabhanga* — which may be translated as ideals of proportion, expression of mood, embodiment of charm, points of view and preparation of colours. The *Vishnu Dharmottara Purana* devotes one full chapter to the art of painting.

Attempts were made to depict the scenes of nature in painting. It is evident from the Chitra Khanda of the *Vishnu Dharmottara Purana*. It contains detailed instructions about the painting of natural scenery. It states that when depiction of six weathers is to be made some important things should be kept in mind by an artist. For example, the summer season is associated with deep wells, tired men, deer searching, shadow of a tree and buffaloes sitting in a dirty pond. Rainy season is associated with a rainbow or an overcast sky, birds resting on branches of trees and the wild animals seeking protection in a cave. This clearly shows that a thorough study of nature was made and an artist was expected to be in full knowledge of nature before depicting any natural scene in a painting.

A Danish artist was so much impressed by the Ajanta paintings that he wrote that "these represent the climax to which genuine Indian art has attained and everything in these pictures from the composition as a whole to the smallest pearl or flower testifies to the depth of insight, coupled with the greatest skill. . .(they are) so accomplished in execution, so consistent in convention, so vivacious and varied in design, and full of such evident delight in beautiful form and colour" that the Ajanta paintings are ranked with the best art of ancient world.[2]

Out of old tradition of painting is born the Rajput art tradition, the Kotah painting, the Kishangarh painting, the Kangra tradition and such other traditions.

Painting has been so popular in India that even now in villages we find instances of wall-painting and painting on ground prevalent. This art of painting is very popular in ladies. One thing that deserves our attention is the fact that the device of preparing lasting colours was so perfected that even the ancient painting despite a gap of thousands of years are still visible. It has not been possible for modern science even to prepare such lasting colours.

Music — Part of Indian Culture

Music has been given due importance in Indian culture. Lord Krishna declares in the *Bhagvadgita*, "I am the *Sama Veda* so far as the Vedas are concerned" (X-22). The *Sama Veda* is concerned with music. This implies that knowledge should result in devotion and human mind finds its greatest joy in music. Bharata's *Natya-shastra* gives us fine information about music. Vocal and instrumental music both have been mentioned there. Narada's *Sangita-Makaranda*, Sarangadeva's *Sangita-ratnakara*, Ahobila's *Sangita-Parijataka*, Damodara's *Sangita-darpana*, Govinda Dixit's *Sangita-sudha* are other works dealing with music. Somanatha's *Ragavibodha* contains a description of different *Ragas*, musical modes and includes 50 pieces of the author's own compositions. The cult of devotion that developed in every province of India gave new impetus to music. Tukarama in Maharashtra, Chaitanya in Bengal and Thyagaraja in South played important roles in popularising music through their devotional compositions.

The *Yajnavalkya Smriti* declares: "That person gets liberation without any effort who knows the secret of playing on the Veena and understands the *talas.*" Although classical music in India differs from region to region, there is an underlying current of unity. India always had unity in diversity because the Vedic literature had been the fountainhead of diverse tendencies found in India.

At present there are two systems of music in India, the Karnataka and the Hindustani. Then we have folk music, *bhajana* and *kirtanas.*

Indian music gives utmost importance to ragas. A *raga* is a melodic scheme covered by some traditional rules, at the same time leaving due freedom for performance. These rules determine the notes of a scale of each *raga*, their order, and their essence which give a particular colour to the scheme. The basic character of Indian music is its emphasis on melody. As a *raga* is a melodic idea, it has to be elaborated to yield its aesthetic potentiality. The seed of the *raga* is present in the *Sama Veda* itself. The *ragas* are based on the time theory. Every *raga* has its particular period of performance. Thus there are the morning *ragas*, the mid-day *ragas*, the dusk *ragas* and the night and mid-night *ragas.* Corresponding to *ragas*, there are *raginis*, which are softer than the *ragas.*

Indian music also gives importance to *tala.* A *tala* is a rhythmic cycle. *Talas* have a universal unity. *Dhrupada* is the most ancient form of musical composition.

Indian music has its instruments. The flute, *vina, mridangam*, plain drum are some of the ancient instruments of music in India. The musical instruments are of four kinds—*tata, sushira, avanaddha* and *ghana.* These distinctions have been made on the basis of their construction. These instruments make music very melodious and pleasant. *Vina* is the most ancient and important instrument of Indian music. It has been mentioned in the ancient literature. *Vina* is associated with Saraswati, the goddess of learning, and the sage Narada. Krishna used to play on flute *(vanshi).* Lord Shiva plays on *Damaru.* Different instruments have been prescribed for different occasions, e.g. on auspicious occasions a specific type of musical instrument is used, while at funeral a different type of instrument is used. A different set of instruments is used to inspire soldiers who march for a battle.

The importance of music in Indian life can be judged from the historical evidence. The *Ganas* or devotees of Shiva are carved out playing with various musical instruments in the Shiva temple of Bhumrah. A dancing woman is engraved on a huge piece of stone at Saranatha. She is surrounded by numerous maidens playing very attractively on many musical instruments like flute, trumpets, etc. Paintings in the Bagh Caves depict two groups of maidens dancing and playing on instruments.

It is thus clear that the art of singing and playing on musical instruments of many types flourished in India from the very beginning of its culture. Even the recital of the Vedas is musical.

Dance—An Ancient Art

Movement accompanied with suggestive gestures is dance. It is an ancient art. Even in the Mohen-jo-daro excavations one bronze idol of a dancing girl was found. Bharata's *Natya-shastra* that was composed in the 1st century A.D. gives a vivid and elaborate description of dance. A systematic exposition of dance in the *Natya-shastra* implies that the art of dance was known to India in her dim past. Lord Shiva is known as *Nata-raja*. His dance is a symbol of both creation and destruction. The association of dance with Shiva suggests that it has spiritual and religious significance. In ancient India, the art of dancing occupied a significant place in social decorum. It was considered desirable for a prince to be well-versed in dance. The *Mahabharata* tells us that Arjuna taught art of dancing to Uttara, the daughter of King Virata. The *Rasa-Lila* of Krishna was a kind of dance that evoked spiritual joy and happiness.

Indian dance has many forms and styles: *Bharatanatyam, Kathakali, Kuchipudi, Manipuri, Yakshagana, Odissi, Kathaka (Katthaka), Chhau*, etc. A dance contains three parts, namely *nritta, nritya* and *natya. Nritta* implies a mere movement of body; *nritya* implies bodily movement accompanied by expression of sentiments; and *natya* implies use of words along with movement of body and expression of emotions and sentiments. That is why it has been accepted that the culmination of the art of dance is attained in a drama.

Kathaka is popular in northern India, *Kathakali* in Kerala, *Kuchipudi* in Andhra Pradesh, *Yaksha Gana* in Karnataka, *Odissi* in

Orissa. Thus India has a rich heritage of the art of dance. Besides these classical dances, India abounds in many types of folk dances.

Although the art of dance occupied a very high position in ancient India because of its association with God and religion, it became degraded in the Moghul and British periods of Indian history. However, due to the efforts of persons like Uday Shankar, Rukmini Devi, Krishna Aiyyar and Rabindranath Thakur, it is regaining its old glory and importance.

We have already discussed poetry of India in earlier pages. We can conclude on the basis of evidences before us that India is rich with all types of art in ample measure. The pleasure derived from the reading of a poem is considered to be equal to the bliss of the attainment of God *(Brahmananda-sahodara)*. There cannot be any better tribute to art.

The artist was given full freedom to express himself in a natural manner. Mammata, in his classic work *Kavya Prakasha* enlightens us on the four characteristic features of art, namely, it is free from all restraints, it is full of joy, it is not dependent on others and it contains ever-new sweetness.

Art has been given so much importance in India that an individual devoid of artistic aptitude is considered to be an animal. Bhartrahari writes that a person lacking an artistic taste is not fit to be called a man; he is an animal devoid of horns and a tail. The Supreme Being has been described as "Kavi" (poet or artist) by the Upanishads. The *Bhagavadgita* informs us that the Lord is poet Ushana(X-37). Thus art occupies a very important position in Indian culture.

NOTES

1. *A History of English Literature*, p.350.
2. *The Paintings of the Buddhist Caves of Ajanta*, p.7.

4

ASTRONOMY, ASTROLOGY AND OTHER SCIENCES

HUMAN INTELLIGENCE expresses itself in kindred forms. If it expresses itself in the forms of poetry, painting, etc., in the domain of art, it expresses itself in the form of the development of various sciences too.

Arithmetic which is the foundation of science was well developed even in the Upanishadic period. The *Chhandogya Upanishad* informs us that Narada had mastered even this science of mathematics. The system of performance of sacrifices indicates the development of geometry. In the ancient India the theory of zero and the consequent development of decimal system too took shape. Aryabhatta, Varahamihira and Brahmagupta were in their own days "the foremost astronomers and mathematicians of the world".

Varahamihira mentions the names of astronomers. Latadeva, Simha, Pradyumna, Vijayanandin and Aryabhatta are present in that list of astronomers. He also gives an account of Siddhantas known as Paitamaha, Romaka, Paulisa, Vashishtha and Surya.

Aryabhatta is the foremost scientist of India of the ancient period. He explains the real causes of solar and lunar eclipses. He states that the eclipses are not caused by Rahu and Ketu. They are caused by the shadow of the earth falling on the moon. His measurement of the earth comes quite close to the modern measurement of the earth. He was the first Indian astronomer who declared that the earth rotates round its axis. He was the first scientist who treated mathematics as a distinct subject and dealt with evolution and involution, area and volume, progression and algebraic identities, and indeterminate equations of the first degree. Aryabhatta is even now famous for his system of notation, which is based on the decimal place-value system, acceptable to the modern world. His three works are *Aryabhattiya, Dasugitika, Sutra* and one not so famous work. The *Aryabhattiya* deals with arithmetic geometry, algebra and trigonometry.

Brahmagupta was such a talented astronomer that long before Newton, he found out the law of gravity. Works of Brahmasiddhanta deal with matters like "arithmetical operations, square and cube-roots, rule of three, interest, progressions, geometry including treatment of the "rational right-angled triangle and the elements of the circle, elementary mensuration of solids, shadow-problems, negative and positive quantities, cipher, surds, simple algebraic identities, indeterminate equations of the first and second degrees which are briefly treated. But special attention has been given to the treatment of cyclic quadrilaterals.

Bhaskaracharya is too well known to need any introduction. His classic work is *Siddhanta-shiromani.* It has been divided in four parts – Lilavati, Bijaganita, Grahaganita and Gola. The first two parts are concerned with mathematics while the latter two are concerned with astronomy. Lilavati has a very interesting way of dealing with mathematical problems.

Rationale Behind Indian Months

Indians had a thorough knowledge of *Nakshatras*, the movements of the moon and sun, changes of seasons, and had measurements of the year and month. The sages of the Vedic period used to perform sacrifices and other such rites at auspicious times. That is why they developed a good knowledge of the movements of stars, planets and the sun. Indians had fixed the names of months on a scientific basis. When the Purnima was associated with the *nakshatra Chitra*, the month was called *Chaitra*, when the *Purnima* was associated with the *nakshatra Vishakha*, the month was called *Vaishakha*, when the *Purnima* was associated with the *nakshatra Jyeshtha*, the month was called *Jyeshtha*, when the *Purnima* was associated with the *nakshatra Purvashada* or *Uttarashadha*, the month was called *Ashadha*, when the *Purnima* was associated with the *nakshatra Shravana*, the month was called *Shravana*, when the *Purnima* was associated with the *nakshatra Purvabhadrapada* or *Uttarabhadrapada*, the month was called *Bhadrapada*, when the *Purnima* was associated with the *nakshatra Ashvina*, the month was called *Ashvina*, when *Purnima* was associated with the *nakshatra Krittika*, the month was called *Kartika*, when the *Purnima* was associated with the *nakshatra Mrigashira*, the month was called *Margashira*, when the *Purnima* was associated with the *nakshatra Pushya*, the month was called *Pausha*, when the *Purnima* was associated with the *nakshatra Magha*, the month was called *Magha*, and when the *Purnima* was associated with the *nakshatra Purvaphalguni* or *Uttaraphalguni*, the month was called *Phalguna*. No such rationale exists behind the names of Western months.

Indians had their own names for the days, viz. *Ravivara, Somavara, Mangalavara, Budhawara, Guruvara, Shukravara* and *Shaniwara*. These names have been kept after the names of planets. This very scheme was borrowed by the West without understanding the reason of the particular names.

It has been accepted by many scholars that Indian scientific works reached Europe via the Arabs and influenced their mind. Of course, the scientific advancement based on mathematics reached a phenomenal height in the West in the course of time. The Indians though precursors and pioneers of science and mathematics lagged behind subsequently due to historical reasons.

Besides astronomy, Indians had developed other sciences too: Archery *(Dhanurveda)*, science of horses *(Ashvashastra)*, science of medicine and surgery *Chikistashastra)*, science of building aeroplanes *(Vaimaniki)*, science of love *(Kama-shastra)*, science of jewels, etc. Ancient India knew many types of weapons that were used in the warfare: *Agneyastra, Parjanyastra, Vayavyastra, Pannagastra, Brahmastra, Pashuptastra, Vaishnava-narayanstra* are the names of some of the powerful weapons that were used at the time of war. Besides *Dhanusha* and *Bana*, there were some other weapons like *Shakti, Tomara, Pasha, Rishi* (a kind of sword), *Gada, Mudgara, Chakra, Vajra, Trishula, Shula, Asi* (sword), *Kbadga, Chandrahasa, Parigha, Bhindipala, Parashu*, etc.

In the *Ramayana* there is mention of an aeroplane called "*Pushpaka*". Rama used it to reach Ayodhya in time. *Vimana* has been described as a vehicle capable of moving on earth, water and sky in a uniform manner like birds *(prithivyapysvantarriksheshu khagvat vegatah svayam yah samartho bhaved gantum sa vimana iti smritah)*.

Even the works dealing with the science of aeroplane were written. In this context the names of such six works have come down to us – *Vimana-chandika, Vyomayanatantra, Yantrakalpa, Yanabindu, Khetayanapradipika.*

Science of jewels was quite developed in ancient India. Jewels are connected with astrology, too, besides being ornaments. The *Agni-purana* contains the matter of examination of jewels in its 245th chapter. Many names of jewels are mentioned there. Some of the names are *Vajra, Marakata, Padmaraga, Mukta, Mahanila, Indranila, Vaidurya, Gandhashasya, Chandrakanta, Suryakanta, Sphatika, Pulaka, Karketana, Pushparaga, Jyotirasa, Rajapatta, Rajamaya, Shankha, Gomeda,* etc., according to the Shukraniti, *Vajra* (diamond), *Mukta, Vaidurya, Gomeda,* etc., are nine principal jewels. *Kamasutra* of Vatsyayana presents the science of love. The work is divided in seven parts. The first part deals with general matters; the second part deals with modes of enjoying love; the third part discusses relations with maidens, giving hints for courtship; the fourth deals with relations with married women; the fifth discusses relations with the women of others; the sixth deals with courtesans; and the seventh deals with the preparation of secret potions to secure love. *Kamasutra* was not written to corrupt young minds; it was written to give scientific information about sex life. Besides *Kamasutra*, other works were also composed.

Science of polity was also much developed in ancient India as is evident from the *Arthashastra* of Chanakya. It lays down the guiding principles of government. The king has certain duties which have been discussed in this classic work. The following quotations may give an idea about the type of the teachings contained in the work:

> "In the happiness of his people lies the happiness of the king, in their well-being his well-being; his own pleasure is not the king's well-being, but the pleasure of his people is his well-being."
> "Even as what lies on the tongue, be it honey or poison, cannot but be tasted, so a little at least of the royal gold that a minister handles must be savoured by him."
> "Men of action achieve their ends, even if it costs hundreds of efforts; wealth is won by wealth as elephants by decoy elephants."

The science of logic also was much developed. The development of logic shows that the Indians were not guided solely by emotions and sentiments. We shall have an occasion to discuss this matter when we discuss the philosophical schools of India. The occult science of astrology was also much developed in ancient period. Astrology is a study of the influence of heavenly stars on human life and the world. Astrology is considered to be the eyes of the Vedas *(vedasya nirmalam chakshurjyotishastramakalmasham).*

Not a Superstition

Astrology is no superstition in India. Human actions can be divided in to three categories: *sanchita, kriyamana* and *prarabdha*. The effect of our acts is not seen immediately. It becomes accumulated. This accumulation is called *sanchita; kriyamana* stands for those acts which are being performed by a person presently; and *prarabdha* suggests the probable effects of our accumulated actions. Just as after a study of the nature of a person, we can say that he would most probably behave in a particular manner, in the same way astrology tells us about the future results on the nature of his past acts mirrored in the horoscope. Varahamihira, a scholar of astrology, states: "Like the night without a light, like the sky without the sun, even so the king without an astrologer wanders blindly on his way."

Varahamihira himself has mentioned that astrologers like Asita Devala, Garga, Vriddha Garga, Narada and Parashara flourished before him. *Brihatsamhita, Horashatpanjika, Horashastra, Vriddha Vashishtha Samhita, Samudratilaka, Svapnachintamani*, etc., are well-known works on astrology.

The *Chhandogya Upanishad* (7-1-2) mentions astrology as one of the major sciences. The *Vishnu Purana* (3-7, 28, 29) includes astrology in one of the 18 vidyas.

Astrology is even now a flourishing science in India. It gives an enlightened guidance to people. Of course, astrology is not fatalism, because it is possible to change the probable influence through efforts and prescribed techniques.

Science of medicine had been very much developed in India. Both treatment of diseases through medicines and surgery were known to ancient India. Charaka, Sushruta and Vagbhata are the outstanding writers on medical science. The science of treatment has been called Ayurveda. The twin aims of Ayurveda are the protection of health of healthy persons and curing the ailment of the unhealthy persons. The basis of both these is life *(ayu)*. Life is very valuable. It is needed even for the attainment of spiritual liberation not to say about he enjoyment of the world. Hence Ayurveda is the science of protection and enhancement of life.

In India a medical practitioner was given due respect. Doctor is supposed to be God on earth *(vaidyo narayano hari)*. Mind and body are the basis of life. The diseases have been divided into four categories, viz. *aguntaka, sharirika, manasika* and *swabhavika*. *Agantuka* diseases are the hurts caused by outside instruments like a weapon, stone, stick, etc.; *sharirika* diseases are ailments of body caused due to defects of food or disturbance of bodily equilibrium;

manasika diseases are caused due to mental reasons and swabhavika diseases are natural events like hunger, thirst, sleep, old age and death.

The duties of a doctor have been prescribed. He is to devote himself fully to his work, even if his own life is at stake; he should never cause any harm to a patient, never entertain evil thoughts as to his wife or goods; to be grave and restrained in demeanour, to devote himself in word, thought and deed to the healing of his charge, not to report outside affairs, and to be careful to utter anything that may retard the recovery of the patient. Ayurvedic preparations are based on the study of the herbs. They are, therefore, generally free from any reaction. The Ayurvedic treatment is based on the principle that the health of an individual depends on the equilibrium of *vata, pitta* and *kapha*, that are present in human body.

The Ayurvedic treatment is becoming more and more popular even in modern Europe because of its effectiveness and absence of side effects. It is really unfortunate that this great system of treatment has been neglected. But the defects of the modern allopathic treatment have forced people to turn to Ayurveda.

5

SOCIAL PHILOSPHY

SOCIAL PHILOSOPHY plays an important role in the making of any society and in giving it a specific shape and form. It will be worth while to understand the outstanding features of social philosophy of ancient India in order to be able to understand the specific nature of Indian culture.

It is evident from a perusal of the Vedic literature that the whole earth was considered one big family *(vasudhaiva kutumbakam)*. A man of knowledge used to think, "Earth is my mother, I am the son of mother earth" *(mata prithvi, putro' ham prithvyah)*. The *Mahabharata* informs us that in the beginning all people were alike and no distinction of any type existed in society. This is not a philosophical dictum alone, it is a fact. Unfortunately, man has forgotten this fact and thinks that the various distinctions that are found at present have been existing from the very beginning.

A perusal of the *Purusha Sukta* of the *Rig Veda* makes it clear that the *Virat Purusha* mentioned therein is actually the human society.

No Caste Distinctions

There were no caste distinctions. Even the names of the four castes in their present sense are not present in the *Rig Veda*. The term "Brahmana" means one who sings the glories of gods, in the *Rig Veda*. "(O frogs) who speaking like the singers of glory in the *Atiratra* sacrifice are proceeding towards the ponds." (R.V. VII.103.7) This hymn makes this point clear. The term "Vipra" occurring in the *Rig Veda* stands for a wise man. The term "Kshatriya" means strong or brave person and refers without any distinction to gods and men in the *Rig Veda*.

There was certainly no division of society even on the basis of profession, not to say about birth or lineage. Persons followed any profession of their linking. A person used to act as carpenter, blacksmith, weaver, sailor, tiller of land, shepherd, etc. In a single family, persons followed different professions suiting their individual likings. One hymn makes this point quite clear:

> "I am a composer of hymns, my son is a physician, and my mother a grinder (of fried barley) on stones. We are of many professions." (Rig Veda IX.112.3)

It is thus clear that society was absolutely free from distinctions of caste or creed.

Four Varnas

But gradually distinctions of professions grew. Even then there was no linking of profession with birth or lineage. It was the distinct likings of persons which prompted them to follow professions of their linking. The *Bhagavadgita* states that the people follow professions because of their distinct tendencies and the consequent actions *(guna-karma vibhagashah)*. There is no mention of birth or lineage in the context of professional distinctions. The 18th chapter of the *Gita* tells us that a person who is interested in learning is a Brahmin, a person who is interested in bodily strength and fearlessness is a Kshatriya, a person who is interested in agriculture, business, etc., is a Vaishya and a person interested in service is a Shudra. But all types of works are equally important. This freedom given to an individual to choose his own profession is quite proper, because modern psychology tells us that such a person gets job-satisfaction and can do his work in an efficient manner.

In order to show that every type of work has its own importance the concept of *Virat Purusha* has been introduced. The Brahmin is the head of this *Purusha*, the Kshatriya is the arm of this *Purusha* the Vaishya is the stomach of this *Purusha* and the Shudra is the feet of this *Purusha*. They are all organically connected like the different parts of human body. Efficiency of human body depends on the health and cooperation of every part. There is no question of the superiority of any part, because every part has a distinctive role to play. every person is advised to follow the profession of his liking but is further advised to do his job in an honest and efficient manner. It is not the nature of the job which is important; it is the honesty, integrity and efficiency of a person that is important. Everybody must understand the importance of his action and the fact that he acts for the entire organism of society. If harmonious relationship does not exist in the different parts of social organism, the organism shall perish, and along with the end of the organism, there will be an end of the organ too. Thus honesty in the performance of one's duty is in the interests of the person himself.

This type of classification of society on the basis of profession has no connection with birth or lineage and contributes to the prosperity of a society. Even Plato had stated that there are three classes in a well-ordered society – rulers, soldiers and artisans. That State is the best in which all these three parts function in a harmonious way.

The *Jati* system came in Hindu society later on because of the inability of its members to understand the meaning and importance of Varna, which was originally based on "varana" (choice) and not on birth.

Even in the modern period a well-ordered society has its varnas, working in a smooth manner.

Four Purusharthas

Indian culture envisaged four supreme ends of human life. These are *Dharma, Artha, Kama* and *Moksha.* These ends imply a synthesis of temporal and spiritual ambitions of a man. *Dharma* stands for both religion and duty. Life should begin from an initiation into dutifulness. The first lesson that was taught was righteousness. After righteousness, i.e. the knowledge of what is right and wrong, one should try to earn money, because without money, life cannot be led properly. Hence, the second aim of man should be to earn money. That is why *Artha* is supposed to be the second end of life. But it is to be remembered that this money has to be earned in the right way. The first end of life, *Dharma*, should never be forgotten. When money is earned, naturally human aspirations and desires should be fulfilled. Hence *Kama* (desire) is the third end of life. But there is still another and ultimate end that is to be achieved. It is *Moksha* or liberation. Death is a certainty, and according to Indian philosophy, if our worldly cravings stick to our mind, we have to take another birth. Hence, it is necessary that something is done whereby the circle of birth and death may be put to an end for ever. This is the state of liberation. Thus life begins with *Dharma* and ends with *Moksha. Artha* and *Kama* are concerned with this very physical world, but *Dharma* and *Artha* are connected with spiritual life. This scheme of four *Purusharthas* is very rational. If this scheme is implemented in life, both society and an individual shall be come happy. At present merely *Artha* and *Kama* are the supreme ends of life. As everybody is running after them, there is a lot of conflict and struggle. This can be ended only if the scheme of four *Purusharthas* is accepted.

Thus the Indian mind acted very wisely by accepting the four supreme ends of life, thereby proving that it had a very balanced view of life and had a capacity of weighing different values in an appropriate manner.

Four Ashramas

Indians had divided human life in four *Ashramas* – *Brahmacharya, Grahstha, Vanaprastha, Sanyasa*. Every *Ashrama* was limited to 25 years. Thus human life was expected to last for at least 100 years on an average. It is quite proper to expect a longevity of 100 years, because in that period, people led very simple and thoughtful life. Their diet was proper, they kept their minds free from worries. Even now a life which is simple and free from worries can easily complete a period of 100 years.

The first *Ashrama* was *Brahmacharya Ashrama*. During this *Ashrama* period, a person used to be solely devoted to the earning of learning. This is the most fruitful period for learning values of life and picking up the essential knowledge of all those things which are needed in life. The second *Ashrama* was *Grahstha Ashrama*. During this period a man used to marry and beget children. The third *Ashrama* was *Vanaprastha*. In this period a person used to think about the spiritual values. And the last *Ashrama* was *Sanyasa Ashrama*. *Sanyasa Ashrama* does not necessarily mean retiring to a forest. It merely means abandonment of worldly desires. If these desires are abandoned, mind becomes calm and quiet. A mind which is calm and quiet at the time of death leads a person to liberation.

The underlying idea behind this scheme of life was to give proper importance to both the worldly life and spiritual values. This scheme saved society from unemployment, because a person would vacate his post voluntarily in favour of others. Society moreover was spared the conflict between the young and the old as is witnessed at present. At present young people find it difficult to overthrow the old people in power. Hence, the conflict becomes inevitable practically in every field. Society was also saved from corruption because if society has persons who are not swayed by personal material desires and aspirations, then corruption cannot flourish.

Three Types of Obligations

The Shathapatha Brahmana informs us that there are four types of obligations (*rina* or debts) that have to be discharged by every person. These obligations are towards the gods, towards the sages, towards ancestors and towards mankind. But generally three kinds of obligations have been accepted in Indian culture. They are called *Pitra rina, Rishi rina* and *Deva rina.*

Pitra rina: Everybody owes a debt towards the ancestors and parents. His parents have given him birth, protection, nourishment, education and also many other things. His very life and body have been given by his parents. The debt that one owes to one's parents is to produce progeny that will continue the tradition of family.

Rishi rina: This implies that the knowledge that has been given to us has to be imparted to other people. The torch of knowledge must be kept burning. It is possible to do so only if the knowledge received by us is given to other persons who, on their part, shall give it to another generation. Thus the torch of knowledge shall remain burning generation after generation.

Deva rina: This implies performing constructive and good acts. Social welfare acts come in this very category.

The scheme of these three obligations creates a good environment in society. People are reminded about their obligations towards society. If these obligations are kept in mind, social organization shall become strong and prosperous.

Marriage

Marriage is the bed-rock of social organization. According to Indian culture, marriage is an indissoluble bond. The relation of husband and wife is not limited to one life. It extends to several births. Our past acts determine the type of wife we get in this life *(purva-dattasu ya bharya...agre agre dhavati)*. Marriage is a sacrament in India. It is not an agreement that can be put to an end at will. According to the *Apastamba Dharma Sutra*, marriage gives capacity to perform religious rites to a man, because an unmarried person is incomplete. Manu the law-giver is of the opinion that progeny, religious rites, enjoyment and attainment of heaven is possible only with the cooperation of wife. According to the *Smritis*, there are three aims of marriage: religious piety, producing progeny and attainment of enjoyment. The main aim is religious; the attainment of enjoyment is only a secondary objective of marriage. The term "putra" (son) means the protector of father from hell.

Marriage is a bondage which cannot be broken. Some people may think it to be a weakness of Hindu marriage. But actually it is its strong point. Every marriage demands a spirit of adjustment. When husband and wife feel that they have to live together for the whole life, they try to make adjustment. Radhakrishnan has rightly stated that ideal marriages are not wrought in heaven; they are to be made on this very earth.

Eight types of marriage have been recognized viz. *Brahma, Arsha, Prajapatya, Deva, Asura, Gandharva, Rakshasa* and *Paishacha*. These types include every kind of marriage. Even a person who seduces a girl has to accept his responsibility as a husband and must pay due attention to the progeny as well as his wife.

Theory of Action

The *Bhagavadgita* which enjoys the foremost authority in Indian culture states that nobody can remain without doing some action. Man is so constituted that he must do some action. The nature of action may be physical, mental, or spiritual. Man is thus condemned to be active, whether he likes it or not. However, man has been endowed with an element of rationality. If he likes, he can act in a discreet manner; but if he likes, he can act in an indiscreet way too. If he acts in a discreet manner, he can expect to get happiness; but if he chooses to act in an irrational way, he will have to experience unhappiness and agony. The *Mimamsa* school of Indian philosophy is of the opinion that every act generates a specific type of energy which is indestructible in nature. If one does a good act, good energy shall be generated; but if he does a bad act, bad energy shall be generated. Nobody should expect that one can get happiness, even when one does something wrong. Freedom implies liberty to act in any way. But it also implies that one will have to accept the fruits of one's actions – sweet or sour. That is why *Gita* declares that one alone is one's friend or foe. (VI.5)

Man is a builder of his own fortune. Three types of actions exist: *sanchita, kriyamana* and *prarabdha*. *Sanchit* is built by the past actions of a person; *kriyamana* suggests the actions being done presently; and *prarabdha* (fate) is the effect of *sanchita* acts. Thus man builds his own destiny. But man is also free to attain a state of liberation where unhappiness is absent totally and for ever. The *Chanakya Niti Darpana* specifically states that the human being acts himself, the fruit of that action is experienced by himself, he himself roams in this world and he himself earns his liberation [*svayam karma karotyatma svayam tatphalamushnute svayam bhramati sansare svayam tasmadvimuchyate*. (VI-9)]

It is because of his actions that a self has to take another birth. The self has to move from birth to birth, from body to body because of his own actions. And the self can get salvation, freedom from this circle of births and deaths only through his own actions. In the *Rig Veda* this very principle of action was termed *Rit*. It was stated that the entire universe moves on this principle of Rit alone.

Education – Its True Meaning

The Indian view about education is that man is a spiritual animal. The animal in man hides the spirit present in a person. Education, in the real sense of the term, is that process whereby the hidden spirituality is aroused in a person. Once a person gets a knowledge and experience of the spirit, he becomes immortal *(sa vidya ya vimuktaye)*. Merely gaining knowledge of literature or mathematics and such other things is not education. Literacy has to be distinguished from education. Real meaning of education is carving out our spiritual personality. This objective can be attained if the four supreme ends of human life – *Dharma, Artha, Kama* and *Moksha* – are accepted and an attempt is made to express them in one's conduct. Literacy is a means of gaining that knowledge, it is not the end of human life. If the animal tendencies of a person are not transformed, he cannot be called educated. From this standpoint, at present we have a distorted view of education. The Bhagavadgita, therefore states that supreme learning is the learning of spirituality *(adhyatma vidya. vidyanam)*.

Supremacy of Dharma

The great *Mahabharata* states that victory can exist only there where *Dharma* (righteousness) is present. Indians were of the opinion that even politics should be based on *Dharma*. A discussion about the forms of government is useless. The quality of the government is more important than the form of government:

> For forms of government let fools contest
> Whatever is best administered is best. – Alexander Pope

In the same strain, the *Chanakya Niti Darpana* states "Where is happiness to people, if a government is bad?" (VI-14) Many duties have been prescribed for a ruler. It is not important whether the form of government is monarchy or democracy. If a King is as efficient and righteous as Rama, will not people be happy? That is why in Indian culture politics is called Raja-niti, i.e. the ethics of government. If a government is bad, people have every right to overthrow it. King Vena was killed because of his misdeeds. That government is best which gives due protection to good people and curbs the evil tendencies firmly.

Unity of Life

Indians believed that everything that we come across in this universe has some life. Even the inanimate is not inanimate. That is why Indians have respect and love for even natural objects like the trees, water, rivers, mountains, air, sun, moon, etc. This tendency was decried by some people. But modern science is slowly accepting its truth. Ecological problems did not arise in the past India, because of the view that the entire universe contains life and must be preserved.

For example, let us pay attention to the following word of the Hymn to Goddess Earth in the *Atharva Veda:*

> ...The earth is the mother, and I the son of the earth; Parjanya is the father...
>
> Upon the firm, broad earth, the all-begetting mother of the plants, that is supported by law, upon her, propitious and kind, may we ever pass our lives...
>
> The fragrance, O earth, that has arisen upon thee, which the plants and waters hold, which the Gandharvas and the Apsaras have partaken of, with that make me fragrant; not any one shall hate us.
>
> The fragrance of thine which has entered into the lotus, that fragrance, O earth, which the immortals of yore gathered up at

the marriage of Surya, with that make me fragrant; not any one shall hate us.

That fragrance of thine which is in men, the loveliness and charm that is in male and female, that which is in steads and heros, that which is in the wild animals with trunks, the lustre that is in the maiden, O earth, with that do thou bless us; not any one shall hate us.

Rock, stone, dust is this earth; this earth is supported, held together. To this golden-breasted earth I have rendered obeisance. The earth, upon whom the forest-sprung trees ever stand firm, The all-nourishing, compact earth, do we invoke."

The peace chants in India wish peace in the entire world including what we call the inanimate world.

Let us end this account with the philosophy of history according to the Indians. The views of Gandhiji are very pertinent in this context. According to him, human history is a record of the struggle between spiritual and animal tendencies present in the world. In this struggle, the spiritual element is slowly becoming victorious. In the dim past, man was indistinguishable from animal. He eat the flesh of man even. Then he came to the stage of eating flesh of other animals. Thereafter he started growing corn and started filling his stomach with corn-made products. Thus the animal in man is gradually yielding to the spiritual element. This is the view of Indians in general. The *Ramayana* and the *Mahabharata* are the stories of the victory of the good over the evil. *Dharma eva jayate* – righteousness alone gains ultimate victory. This is the lesson of history too. The wheel of history moves gradually in the direction of human unity and amity, destroying the obstacles through conflict and struggle. The world is so constituted that both good and evil are present in it and their constant struggle makes human life meaningful and significant. Tulasidasa has described in his *Ramacharita-manasa* that a society occupying the chariot of rigteousness alone becomes victorious *(sakha dharmamaya asa ratha jaken jitana kaha na katahu ripu taken)*.

This is a very sensible philosophy of history which can inspire people to work for creative forces. It is against Marx's materialistic interpretation of history according to which the economic factor is the sole determiner of movement of history. While the importance of the economic factor cannot be underestimated, it is wrong to put all emphasis on the economic factor alone, because thereby we create an opportunity for a ceaseless bloody struggle to continue for an endless period. What shall be the outcome of such a philosophy in this age of atomic weapons can be understood very easily.

6

PHILOSOPHY, RELIGION AND ETHICS

PHILOSOPHY CAN be defined as a logical and synthetic study of the ultimate truth. The Upanishads call this supreme truth as the Truth of truths *(satyasya satyam)*. This is a correct description of the supreme truth because it has to be distinguished from the smaller truths of our practical life. Whatever comes across our perception appears to be true. But to understand the ultimate truth we shall have to transcend these seemingly real objects.

It must be clearly understood that the term *Darshana* has a distinct meaning. In the West the term philosophy stands for love for knowledge. This love for knowledge takes the Western thinkers to peculiar domains. For example, at present the function of philosophy is just to make a logical analysis of perceptual statements. Philosophy has nothing to do with a study of the ultimate truth. In India the task of *Darshana* is the realization of the ultimate truth. Of course, logical knowledge too has been given due respect because it has been held that liberation is inattainable without knowledge *(rite jnanat na muktih)*. But a mere linguistic approach has no meaning. It cannot take us to our ultimate objective of realization of the supreme truth.

Some Western scholars have a misconception about the philosophy of India. They think that there cannot be any Indian philosophy as such, because India is a continent with many languages, rituals and climates.

But this type of thinking is not right. There are some peculiar features, which are common to every philosophical system of India. This shows that there is Indian philosophy. A brief mention of these common points may be made here.

1. Indian philosophy is practical. According to Indian philosophy, this world is full of misery and unhappiness. Everybody has a share of his agonies. Philosophy is not merely formulating certain theories. It must show us a way to end our agonies. Thus philosophy has a practical motive of leading us to a state of perpetual happiness. That is

why barring the *Charvaka* system, every system of philosophy in India tries to show the path of liberation.

2. Every system has a faith in an eternal moral order. The universe cannot exist without this moral order. The *Rig Veda* gives it the name of *Rita*; the *Mimamsa* School gives it the name of *Apurva;* the *Nyaya Visheshika* call it *Adrishta.* This rule of moral order is so strong that a person cannot escape it even after death. He shall have to be born again in the light of his past actions. The wheel of action shall always be moving till one gets liberation through selfless activities.

3. The universe is thus a moral stage or examination hall where everybody gets an opportunity to act in a way one likes, but where everybody has to suffer the consequences of one's acts.

4. Ignorance of the Supreme Truth is the chief cause of all the evils and sufferings of a person. Knowledge of the Real alone can set a person free from the sufferings.

5. A theoretical knowledge is not enough to gain liberation. Hard practice is needed. One's character has to be developed in a new direction. For this, eight-fold *Yoga* has been prescribed. The practice of Yoga changes the very character and conduct of a man.

6. All schools except the *Charvaka* believe in the law of *karma*. Our actions are freely determined by the self.

7. All schools except the *Charvaka* believe in the reality of the *Atman* (the self). The Bauddhas regard the psychic continuum – *vijnana santana* – as the self. The Jainas agree with *Nyaya Vaisheshika* in regarding the self as an eternal substance.

8. All schools except the *Charvaka* believe in liberation as the highest end of life. *Dharma, Artha* and *Kama* are other three ends of life.

9. There is a close connection between philosophy and religion. The problems of religion stimulate philosophic inquiry. The importance of religion and social tradition does not come in the way of the growth of philosophy in India.

10. As a matter of fact Indian philosophy accepts a distinction of persons from the standpoint of their capacity of understanding truth *(adhikari-bheda)*. The ultimate philosophic truth cannot be understood by a person of ordinary intelligence and taste. All the Indian systems of philosophy are inter related as they proceed from materialism, pluralism and dualism to monism. The *Vedanta* of Shankara may be considered to be the crest of philosophical thinking.

11. All the systems of Indian philosophy are born from the ocean of

the Upanishads which are the store-house of philosophical thought. They are the main sources of Indian systems, whether this fact is clearly accepted or not.

It is clear from the above facts that there is Indian philosophy. Now, it will be worth while to give a short account of all the philosophic schools of India.

On the basis of acceptance of the Vedas as authority, the philosophical schools have been divided into two categories, viz. *Astika* and *Nastika*. Charvaka, Jaina and Bauddha schools are considered *Nastika* while *Nyaya Vaisheshika, Samkhya, Yoga, Mimamsa (Purva Mimamsa)* and *Vedanta (Uttara Mimamsa)* are considered to be *Astika*.

The Charvakas

The *Charvakas* hold that perception is the only valid source of knowledge. All non-perceptual or indirect sources of knowledge like inference, testimony of persons, etc., are unreliable. We should, therefore, accept only that thing as valid which is known or knowable through perception.

If we rely solely on perception, as we should do, we find that only the material world composed of four *bhutas* (elements of matter) is real. Air, fire, water and earth are the elements of matter. All the objects that we find in this world are products of these four elements alone. There is no reason to accept the existence of any immaterial self. Man too is a combination of the four elements. Generally we say, "I am stout", "I am fair", "I am hungry" or any other thing of the type. These judgments denote that the individual is simply body. What we call consciousness, that too is a quality of the living body. Consciousness is produced just as red colour is produced when betel leaf, nut and lime are chewed together, or molasses acquires the power of intoxication when fermentation takes place. Hence consciousness is merely the result of a particular combination of the four elements. When a man dies, nothing is left of him. Hence survival of man in any form after death is impossible. The existence of God too cannot be accepted, as there is no evidence to prove God's existence. The universe is produced by the automatic combination of material elements. Hence, it is irrational to perform any religious rite either for enjoying heavenly bliss or for pleasing God. A rational man, say the *Charvakas*, should not have any faith in the Vedas or the cunning priests. Priests merely befool persons to earn their livelihood.

Therefore, if a man is rational, his highest aim can be only the enjoyment of the greatest amount of pleasure in this world, of which we are sure. It is foolish to think that material pleasures should be discarded because they are mixed with pain. It is as foolish as rejecting the kernel because of its husk or ceasing sowing crops for fear of animals or cattle. Hence, the wisest course is to enjoy life fully. Even if one is required to get money through the so called immoral means, there is no harm in doing so. Let everybody know that when the body is reduced to ashes, nothing remains. It is absurd to talk about the existence of soul, or transmigration of soul or even about God.

The Jaina Philosophy

This system rejects the *Charvaka* view that perception is the only valid source of knowledge. It should not be forgotten that even perception at times proves illusory. While the Charvakas criticise inference, they themselves use inference when they say that all cases of inference are misleading, because how can they observe all the cases of inference? The Jaina system accepts perception, inference and testimony as valid sources of knowledge.

Perception reveals the reality of the material substances, composed of four kinds of elements as stated by the *Charvakas*. Apart from material substances, we shall have to accept the existence of space *(akasha)*, because material substances must exist somewhere, existence of time *(kala)* because changes and successions of substances cannot be understood on the basis of perception, existence of dharma (cause of motion) and existence of a Sharma (cause of rest). Existence of souls is also admitted. The *Charvakas* are wrong when they think that consciousness is the product of matter, because they cannot show even a single case where consciousness has been produced through a combination of material atoms. Further, without a conscious substance to organize them, the body and the senses cannot do their work systematically. But there are innumerable souls – in fact as many souls as there are living bodies. The souls exist not only in animals, but even in plants and the particles of dust.

It should be noted that, according to this system, all souls are not equally conscious. Plants and dust particles have tactual consciousness alone. Some animals have only two senses, others three, and still others four. But Man and other higher animals have five senses. The soul, moreover, has limited knowledge. Its power too is limited. It is stated that despite this fact, every soul is capable of attaining infinite consciousness, power and happiness. These qualities are lying dormant in souls because of the obstruction of *karmas*. Just as the light of the sun is obstructed by clouds, in the same way the natural power of the soul is obstructed by the *karmas*. The *karmas* are actually forces of passions and desires existing in the soul and attract to it particles of matter. Thus the *karmas* are responsible for the bondage of the soul by matter. However, *karmas* can be removed. And when they are removed, the soul's bondage is destroyed and its perfections are experienced.

The teachings of the liberated souls *(tirthankaras)* point to the path of liberation. Three things are essential for the removal of bondage: faith in the teachings of the teachers, correct knowledge of the teachings and right conduct.

Right conduct demands the following of moral codes, e.g. not injuring any life, speaking truth, not indulging in any stealing, abstaining from sensuality and attachment to sensual objects. When the prescribed moral code is practised, the fetter of the soul falls down and the soul attains infinite faith, infinite knowledge, infinite power and infinite bliss.

The Jaina system has no place for God. Tirthankaras are, however, worshipped like God. The system believes that there are many aspects of every object, but an ordinary person can judge any object form his own angle alone. We should not forget that knowledge of every person is thus limited and relative. Hence we should abstain from dogmatic assertion. Thus a theory of relativity in the domain of truth has been advanced by the Jaina thinkers. This suggests a toleration of other theories and views.

The Bauddha Theory

The founder of this system was Gautama Bauddha, who attained the enlightenment after great hardships. He advocated Four Noble Truths, viz. the Truth that there is misery, the Truth that there is a cause of this misery, the Truth that this misery can be ended. The Truth that there is a path that can lead any person to '' is ending of misery.

The first Truth can be accepted by any person because there is no person in this world who has not experienced misery of any type at any time. Misery is universally present. Even what appears to us to be pleasant at present proves ultimately to be a source of pain. The second Truth is based on the theory of causation. Our misery too must be due to some cause. Suffering depends on birth in this world. If a person is not born, he cannot have any occasion of misery. Now, birth is caused by our desire *(trishna)* for the mundane objects. Our desires are caused by our ignorance. If we can have a correct picture of the world, we can understand that everything here is subject to change and decay. We shall then have no desire for the worldly objects. And when there are no desires, there shall be no birth, and when there is no birth, there shall be no misery. The third Truth too is a matter of our experience. Suffering is dependent on some conditions. If the conditions are removed, the suffering too must end.

The fourth Truth is that there is a way of attaining the state of the end of suffering. This path is called the Eight-Fold Noble Path as it consists of eight steps, viz. Right Views, Right Determination, Right Speech, Right Conduct, Right Livelihood, Right Endeavour, Right Mindfulness and Right Concentration. This path has been called *Arya Ashtangika Marga* because it is the path liked by the nobleminded people. If this path is pursued truthfully, ignorance and worldly desires are destroyed and perfect equanimity of mind is attained. The state of perfection, not influenced by any desire and ignorance, has been termed *Nirvana* (liberation) and is attainable in this very life.

Buddha was a practical thinker. He knew that it is essential to remove the misery of the people. Teaching philosophy to every person has no practical significance. That is why he kept silent whenever he was put any philosophical question.

But no rational person can reject philosophical discussion totally. Naturally, therefore, Buddha's teachings contained philosophical theories.

The following philosophical thoughts can be gleaned from his teachings:

(i) All things are conditional.
(ii) All things are subject to change.
(iii) There is neither any soul, nor God, nor any other permanent substance.
(iv) There is, however, birth followed by another due to the result of the acts of a person. It is like the seeds of a tree which give birth to other trees in the course of time.

Although Buddha did not like to present any metaphysical theory himself, his followers built up metaphysical theories on the basis of stray thoughts of their master. The following four theories are the prominent theories that are associated with Buddhism.

(a) *The Madhyamika* or *Shunyavada:* This view holds that the world is unreal (*shunya*). Mental and non-mental phenomena are, therefore, unreal (*shunya*). Because of its emphasis on *shunya*, this theory has been called *Shunyavada*. However it has to be remembered that the term *Shunya* has a specific meaning. The term "sunya" means indescribable. Thus the theory actually implies that the Real is such that it cannot be described. It can be called *Brahmavada* of the Upanishads. But due to the use of the word "shunya", it has been much misunderstood. We should not forget that the Upanishads are the fountainhead of all Indian systems of philosophy.

(b) *The Yogachara* or *Vijnanavada:* This school holds that all external objects are unreal. An outside object is merely an idea in mind. The reality of mind cannot be disputed. It is self-contradictory to state that the mind is unreal; because then the very thought that mind is unreal shall become unmeaningful; thought is after all an activity of the mind itself. If there is no mind, there can be no thought. This view has been given the name of *Vijnanavada* (subjective idealism). According to scholars, like the *Shunyavada*, this theory too has been rather misunderstood.

(c) *The Sautrantika:* This school holds that all the mental as well as non-mental objects are real. Existence of external objects can be inferred from the idea present in our mind. We can have the perceptual idea of an object present before us. Hence, the existence of an object is proved from the perceptual idea. This view is thus the theory of the inferability of external objects *(bahyanumerya-vada).*

(d) *The Vaibhashika:* This school holds that external objects are directly perceived and not inferred from their ideas or representations in the mind. Thus this theory holds that external objects are perceived directly *(bahya-pratyaksha-vada).*

So far as the religion is considered, Buddhism has been divided into two schools, viz. *Hinayana* and *Mahayana.*

The Hinayana is found in Ceylon, Burma and Siam; the Mahayana is present in Tibet, China and Japan. The main difference between these two is that the Hinayana is of the opinion that salvation in individual. A man should strive to attain it so that his miseries may be put to an end for ever. The Mahayana, on the other hand, holds that our aim should be to get salvation for all the people. The *Sautrantika* and the *Vaibhashika* schools belong to the Hinayana sect. On the other hand the *Shunyavada* and the *Yogachara* systems belong to the Mahayana sect of Buddhism.

The Nyaya

The founder of the Nyaya system was a sage named Gotama. This system is realistic and has a very developed logic. According to this system, there are four sources of real knowledge, viz. *pratyaksha* (perception) inference *(anumana)*, *upamana* (comparison) and *shabda* (authority). Perception is of two kinds, viz. external and internal. Inference of objects is obtained through the apprehension of some mark *(linga)* which is invariably connected with the inferred object *(sadhya)*. The invariable connection between the sadhya and the *linga* is called *vyapti*. In every inference there are at least three propositions and at most three terms viz. the *paksha* or minor term, the *sadhya* or major term and the linga or middle term having an invariable relation with the *sadhya* term, and is present in the minor. Let us take an example. "The hill has fire, because there is smoke there; and whatever smokes contains fire."

Upamana is the knowledge of a relation between a name and things so named on the basis of a given description of their similarity to some familiar object. For example, we tell a person that a *gavaya* is found in a forest and resembles a cow, and subsequently when he sees such an animal in the forest, he would immediately conclude that this must be a *gavaya*. *Shabda* is the knowledge about unperceived objects derived from the statements of authoritative persons. For example, a man of science tells us that water is produced due to a compound of hydrogen and oxygen in a certain proportion. This knowledge is accepted because it has come to us from a man of authority. In the domain of religion, this type of knowledge is very much prevalent.

The objects of knowledge are the self, the body, the senses and their objects, cognition *(buddhi)*, mind *(manas)*, activity *(pravritti)*, mental defects *(dosha)*, rebirth *(pretyabhava)*, the feelings of pleasure and pain *(phala)*, suffering *(dukha)* and freedom from suffering *(apavarga)*. The Nyaya believes in the ultimate objective of salvation *(apavarga)*. The self is actually distinct from the body and the mind. The body is a composite substance made of matter. The mind is a subtle, indivisible and eternal substance *(anu)*. It is an instrument of perception of psychic qualities like pleasure, pain, etc. That is why the mind is called an internal sense. The self *(atman)* too is distinct from mind and body. It acquires the attribute of consciousness when it is related to any object through the senses. But it should be clear that, according to the *Nyaya*, consciousness is not an essential quality of the self. It is only its accidental quality which is absent in the self in the state of liberation. Mind is very small like an atom, but the self is all-pervading *(vibhu)*, indestructible and eternal. It is an agent responsible for likes or dislikes of objects. It is also responsible for obtaining or avoiding objects and enjoyments or suffering resulting from the acts. The self is misled by the false knowledge *(mithya-jnana)* which prevents it from obtaining the knowledge of the real. *Raga dvesha, moha* and such other tendencies impel the agent to act and plunge it in the suffering, birth and rebirth and all such other miseries. Liberation is a state where there is a complete cessation of all types of pains and sufferings. This becomes possible because of the right knowledge of the real. The Nyaya does not share this view that liberation is a state of happiness, because there is no pleasure without pain. Pleasure and pain are inter-related like light and shade. Hence, the state of liberation has to be accepted as a state free from both pleasure and pain.

The Nyaya accepts the existence of God and tries to prove God's existence by logical arguments. God is the ultimate cause of the creation, maintenance and destruction of the universe. God has created the universe out of eternal atoms, space, time, ether, minds and selves. The universe has been created so that the selves may reap the fruits of their acts either in the form of pleasure or pain. God is responsible for giving results as per the acts of an individual soul. In the absence of God, who shall see that the individuals get the fruits of their acts? There is still another argument. All objects of the world like mountains and seas, the sun and the moon, are effects because they are composed of parts. Therefore they must have a maker. The individual selves cannot be the creator of the universe, because they are absolutely limited in power and knowledge and, therefore, have no power to deal with subtle and imperceptible entities like atoms whose various combinations give birth to the world, and its objects. Moreover, the creator of the universe must possess unlimited intelligence, power and wisdom and at the same time he must be able to maintain the moral order of the world. God's existence, therefore, must be accepted. Under His loving care and wise guidance, all persons can hope to get right knowledge sooner or later and can attain the state of liberation.

The Vaisheshika

The founder of this system was Kanada *(Uluka)*. This system has much similarity with the Nyaya. It brings all objects of knowledge, i.e. the entire universe, under seven categories. These are: substance *(dravya)*, quality *(guna)*, action *(karma)*, generality *(samanya)*, particularity *(vishesha)*, the relation of inherence *(samavaya)* and non-existence *(abhava)*.

Substance has been described as the substratum of qualities and actions; but at the same time, it is different from both. Substances are of nine kinds viz. earth, water, fire, air, ether, time, space, self and mind. Earth, water, fire, air and ether are called physical elements *(bhutas)*. Each element contains a specific quality, i.e. the quality of earth is smell, the quality of water is taste, the quality of fire is colour, the quality of air is touch, the quality of ether is sound. Earth, water, fire and air are composed of atoms which are indivisible and indestructible. The atoms are uncreated and eternal entities and can be obtained by resolving any material object into smaller and smaller parts till we get such parts as cannot be divided further. *Akasha* (ether), space *(dik)* and time *(kala)* are imperceptible substances, each of which is eternal, all-pervading and one. The mind *(manas)* is an eternal substance which is not all-pervading, but is infinitely small like an atom. *Manas* is an internal sense which is concerned, directly or indirectly, in all physical functions like cognition, feeling and willing. As the mind is atomic, we cannot have more than one experience at a time. The self is an eternal and all-pervading substance and is the substratum of consciousness. The individual self is perceived internally by the mind. This is evident from our experience. For example, we say "I am feeling miserable" or "I am happy". The existence of the supreme soul has to be known through inference. He is the creator of the universe. God creates the universe out of eternal atoms.

The atoms being inert cannot move themselves. The source of their movement is God. God directs the activities of atoms in the light of the law of action. The atoms assume the form and shape in due accordance with the unseen moral deserts *(adrishta)* of the selves and thus create a world of morality. This theory is known as the atomic theory of the *Vaisheshika*. As can be noted, this theory is teleological.

A quality is described as something that exists in a substance and has itself no quality or activity. The difference between a substance and a quality lies in the fact that the substance can exist by itself, while a quality can exist only in some substance. Quality has neither activity nor movement. The Vaisheshika system believes in the existence of 24 kinds of qualities, viz. colour, taste, small, touch, sound, number, magnitude, distinctness, conjunction, disjunction, remoteness, nearness, fluidity, viscidity, cognition, pleasure, pain, desire, aversion, striving, heaviness, tendency, merit and demerit.

An action is a movement. It can exist only in a substance. There are five kinds of action viz. throwing upward, throwing downward, contraction, expansion and going.

Samanya is the eternal essence common to all the individuals of a class just as dogness is common to all dogs. *Samanya* is not born by birth, nor does it die by death. It is everlasting. Particularity is the cause of the ultimate difference of things. Particularity is the source of difference found even in two atoms. No two things can be alike. As this system gives so much importance to particularity *(vishesha)*, it has been called the Vaisheshika philosophy.

Inherence is the permanent relation by which a whole exists in its parts. The cloth as one whole exists in the threads. *Samavaya* is thus a permanent relation existing between the whole and its parts, between the universal and its individuals and between qualities or actions and their substances. Non-existence *(a-bhava)* is also real. It stands for all negative facts. "This cow is not white", "This water is not pure" and such other propositions express the non-existence of something. All such cases of non-existence come under the category of *a-bhava*. It has four kinds viz. *pragabhava, dhvansabhava, atyantabhava*, and *anyonyabhava*. *Pragbhava* means the non-existence of a thing before its production, e.g. the non-existence of a pot in clay before its production; *dhvansabhava* means the non-existence of a thing after its destruction, e.g. non-existence of a pot after its being broken into pieces; *atyantabhava* means absence of a relation between two things for all time, e.g. non-existence of colour in the air; *anyonyabhava* means the absolute difference of one thing from another, e.g. a piece of cloth is different from a piece of a stone. When two things differ, there is the non-existence of either as the other. Thus mutual non-existence of two different things is known as *anyonyabhava*. The *Vaisheshika* is the only philosophical system in the world which has accepted the category of *a-bhava*. So far as God and the question of liberation are concerned the *Vaisheshika* agrees with the *Nyaya* system.

The Samkhya

The founder of this system was *Kapila*. It is a dualistic system of philosophy. *Purusha* and *Prakriti* are two ultimate realities. They are absolutely distinct and dissimilar. The *Purusha* is consciousness *(chaitanya)*. Prakriti is inert and unconscious. Everything that we see in the universe is a form of inert Prakriti. Even our body, senses and the mind are forms of Prakriti. All physical objects like chair, table, etc., exist for the enjoyment of beings other than themselves. This proves the existence of the Purusha (the self) which is distinct from Prakriti. Purushas are many because when some persons are happy others are unhappy, some persons die, but others enjoy. Therefore many Purushas related to different bodies have definite existence.

Prakriti is the ultimate cause of the world. It is constituted by *Sattva, Rajas* and *Tamas* elements. In the original state, all the three constituents are in a state of equilibrium. These constituents have been given the name of *Guna*. Thus there are three *Gunas*, viz. *Sattva, Rajas* and *Tamas*. The existence of the *Gunas* is inferred from the qualities of pleasure, pain and indifference which are present in all the objects of the world. A mango may be liked by some, disliked by some; and there may be some persons who are indifferent to it. Not only this, the same sweet is liked or disliked or treated with indifference by the same person in different conditions. The *Samkhya* holds the theory of *Satkaryavada* according to which the cause and effect are essentially identical. The effect is the manifested state of the cause. For example, oil is merely a manifested condition of the seeds. The objects of the world are effects having the qualities of pleasure, pain and indifference. Hence, the Prakriti *(Pradhana)* being their ultimate cause must have the three elements of *Sattva, .Rajas* and *Tamas*, which respectively possess the natures of pleasure, pain and indifference.

The evolution of the world takes place because of the proximity of Purusha. The evolution takes place in Prakriti because it is subject to changes, while the Purusha is beyond any change. The first evolute is *Mahat*. From *Mahat* is born *Ahankara*. From *Ahankara* are born mind, five sense organs, five motor organs and five *tanmatras*; and from *tanmatras* are born five *mahabhutas*, i.e. the entire concrete physical world. It should be remembered that even mind is an evolute of Prakriti.

Individual self is quite distinct from the Prakriti and its evolutes; but because of ignorance of the truth, the self identifies itself with the body and other external things and feds unhappiness at the changes taking place in their domains. Thus it should be clear that indiscrimination is the real cause of sorrows and sufferings. Once we realize the distinction between the self and not-self such as the body, the senses, the mind, the intellect and the ego, our self shall cease to be affected by the joys and sorrows and the changes taking place in the world.

Once this discrimination dawns, a person becomes a dispassionate observer of the events. This is a state of liberation which has been given the names like *mukti, apavarga, kaivalya*, etc. It is possible to attain this state while alive. This is called *Jivana-mukti.* When in due course of time, body falls down, a person attains *Videha-mukti.* But this liberation cannot be attained only by the attainment of oral knowledge. One needs a thorough spiritual discipline to transform one's life and conduct.

There are two versions of the Samkhya – one that gives no importance to God because God's existence cannot be proved, nor do we need any God to explain the origin of the world. But there is another section that accepts God, because there must be some connecting link between Prakriti and Purusha. But generally it is held that the Samkhya does not accept any God.

The Yoga

The founder of the Yoga system was Patanjali. It is closely allied to the Samkhya. It accepts the epistemology and metaphysics of the Samkhya. But unlike the *Samkhya, Yoga* admits the existence of God. But the most important aspect of this system is to provide the path of discipline that can lead a person to the attainment of spiritual objective. The *Yoga* has been defined as the cessation of all mental modifications *(chittavrattinirodha).* For this purpose five levels of mind have been distinguished. The first is known as *kshipta* being the condition in which mind flirts among objects. The second is known as *mudha* in which mind is in the condition of sleep. The third is known as *vikshipta* which is a condition of, relatively speaking, peace. These three conditions are not suitable for spiritual attainment. The fourth is called *ekagra* which is a condition of mental concentration. The fifth is known as *niruddha* which is a condition in which mind is free even from the act of contemplation. These two states of mind are suitable for Yoga.

There are two kinds of *Samadhi-yoga*, viz. *samprajnata* and *a-samprajnata*. In the samprajnata, we have mind's perfect concentration on the object of contemplation; while in *asamprajnata* state there is a complete stoppage of all mental modifications.

The *Yoga* system prescribes eight steps for spiritual upliftment: *Yama* (restraint), *Niyama* (ethical culture), *Asana* (bodily posture), *Pranayama* (breath control), *Pratyahara* (withdrawal of senses from sense objects), *Dharana* (attention), *Dhyana* (meditation) and *Samadhi* (concentration).

The Yoga accepts God and states that He is the highest object of contemplation. God is the perfect being and is eternal, all-pervading, omniscient, omnipotent and perfect. The grounds for the acceptance of God too have been adduced. Whatever has degrees must have a maximum. There are degrees of knowledge; therefore, there must be such a thing as perfect knowledge or omniscience. The being who has omniscience is God. Still further, Prakriti and Purusha are quite distinct and dissimilar substances. They cannot come together themselves. God unites and disunites them causing creation and destruction respectively. Hence, God is that being who brings about connection and disconnection between Purusha and Prakriti.

The Mimamsa

The *Mimamsa* is also known as the *Purva Mimamsa* to distinguish it from the Vedanta or the *Uttara Mimamsa*. The founder of this system was *Jaimini*. The primary object of this system is to provide rationalistic foundation for the Vedic ritualism. But in the attempt it builds up its own philosophy.

According to this system, the Vedas are not the works of any person and, therefore, they are free from the errors that are inevitable in human thinking. The Vedas are eternal and self-subsisting. The seers merely manifested them through speech or writing. It advocates the theory of *svatah-pramanyavada*, i.e. the theory of self-evidence of knowledge. When there are sufficient conditions, knowledge comes out. When the senses are healthy, objects are present before them, and other helpful conditions are also available, there is perception. When there are enough data, there is inference. When we read a book of botany, we have knowledge of plants described in it through authority.

Our knowledge mostly comes from such sources of authority, because human life has no capacity to know each and everything. In the same way, the knowledge of the ultimate truth can be derived on the basis of authority alone. The Vedas are such authorities. The validity of the Vedic knowledge is self-evident.

Right *(dharma)* is that which has been commanded by the Vedas. What has been forbidden by them is wrong *(a-dharma)*. Duty consists in doing those acts which have been permitted by the Vedas. The rituals recommended by the Vedas should be performed merely because they are Vedic commandments and not out of any hope for reward. Disinterested performance of the obligatory acts destroys the karmas and bestows liberation after death. The state of liberation is the state of absolute bliss or heaven. But later writers conceive liberation merely as stoppage of all births and consequent pains.

The soul is immortal. However, consciousness is not the intrinstic quality of the self. Consciousness arises in the self only when it becomes associated with body and still further when an object is presented to the organs of knowledge. In the state of liberation, the self has no body and, therefore, it has no consciousness. But the potentiality of consciousness is present in the self. The *Mimamsa* accepts five sources of valid knowledge, viz. perception *(pratyaksha)*, inference *(anumana)*, comparison *(upamana)*, testimony *(shabda)* and postulation *(arthapatti)*. Kumarila Bhatta, a well-known author of the system, admits even a sixth source. It has been called non-cognition *(anupalabdhi)*. The *Mimamsa* system accepts the reality of the physical world. It also accepts the reality of the self. But it does not accept the existence of God. According to this system, the law of *karma* rules the world. When any person performs any ritual, there arises in his self a potency *(apurva)* which produces in future the fruit of the action at the proper time. This theory of Apurva can be applied to every type of work. The result of the work cannot be avoided by any person. There is no necessity of God. The principle of Apurva is sufficient to explain the fruits of actions.

The Vedanta

This system is also known as *Uttara Mimamsa*. It has arisen from the Upanishads which are the culmination of the fine philosophical speculative thought in India. The term Vedanta also implies that this knowledge is the highest knowledge.

The *Rig Veda* tells us about the fact that there is only one single Truth present in the universe; this very Truth has been described by different persons in different ways. This very Truth has been described as the Brahman or the Atman in the Upanishads. All is God *(sarvam khalu idam Brahma)* : this Self is Brahman *(ayam Atma Brahma)*; there is no multiplicity here *(neha nanasti kimchana)*. This is the declaration of the Upanishads.

Shankara, the great *Acharya* of Indian philosophy, built up his theory of Kevaladwaitavada on the basis of the writings found in the Upanishads.

The Advaita system of philosophy is thus based on the teachings of the Upanishads. In Indian philosophy only that scholar was given the status of Acharya who proved that his view is supported by the Upanishads, the *Brahma-sutra* of Badarayana Vyasa and the *Bhagavadgita*. Hence the great Acharyas of Indian philosophy wrote commentaries on all these three works to prove that the views held by them have the support of these three works. It will be worth-while to acquaint ourselves with the views of prominent Acharyas who influenced the philosophy and religion of India.

Shankaracharya

The first and foremost Acharya is Shankara. He was not only a great scholar, he was also a man of philosophical genius. His arguments are so weighty that even after passing of so many long years after his death, world has not produced any philosophical genius equal to him.

Shankara tells us that pure monism is the only rational philosophy that can be accepted. The Brahman is the only truth. This Brahman is free from all distinctions, *sajatiya, vijatiya* or *svagata*. The difference between Mohan and James is *sajatiya bheda*; difference between a horse and a deer is *vijatiya bheda* and distinctions of hands, feet, nose, etc., in a human body are *svagata bheda*. What is meant is that the Brahman is free from all types of differences and distinctions. Still further, there is no distinction between the Self *(Atman)* and the Brahman. The Self is actually the Brahman. But because of ignorance, it thinks itself to be the body and the senses and imagines all types of limitations. But when the knowledge of the Real is obtained, a person realizes "I am Brahman".

What about the plurality that a person sees in the world Shankara says that this is a creation of *Maya* (illusion). The world is not totally unreal. There are three levels of existence, viz. *Pratibhasika Satta, Vyavaharika Satta* and *Paramarthika Satta.* When one sees a snake in a piece of rope, it is a case of Pratibhasika Satta. Thus an illusion has Pratibhasika Satta. The world has Vyavaharika Satta, because even when one realizes the Brahman, one has to accept the practical reality of the world. But the Brahman has Paramarthika Satta, because the reality of the Brahman is never sublated. It is noteworthy that Shankara does not consider the world to be an illusion. When the Brahman is associates with Maya, He is God the determinate Brahman. But in the real knowledge the God too disappears. Only the Brahman in its indeterminate from remains. A man of knowledge can realize his Brahmanhood. Shankara is of this opinion that no liberation is possible without knowledge. However knowledge does not mean verbal knowledge. It means knowledge that assumes a concrete from in the shape of actual conduct.

Shankara has given due importance to devotion, which is a great purifier of heart and thus prepares ground for the cultivation of the highest knowledge.

Ramanuja is another important thinker of the Advaita system. But his Advaita is known as Vishishtadvaita, because he thinks that the Jiva and the material world constitute the body of God and they are eternal in their subtle forms. Maya is the wonderful power of God. The Jivas *(chit)* and the Universe *(a-chit)* are real. But they act under the control of God. God can be realized through knowledge that has assumed the form of devotion.

The other thinkers who have advocated their own types of non-dualism are *Madhva, Nimbarka, Vallabha* and *Chaitanya.* All these thinkers have given supreme importance to devotion as a means of God realization.

Besides these thinkers who have been called *Vaishnava,* i.e. the followers of Vishnu as the Supreme Reality, there are Shaiva and Shakta schools.

Perhaps philosophy is nowhere so popular in the world than in India. The *Bhagavadgita* has rightly declared that the foremost science is the science of the Self *(adhyatma-vidya vidyayam).* The credit of popularizing philosophy goes to the saints like Valmiki, Vyasa, Kabiradasa, Tulasidasa, Nanaka, Alwara saints, Chaitanya and a host of other saints too innumerable to be mentioned here. Thanks to these saints, even a farmer working in a field, even a worker working in a factory, nay even a beggar can talk about the philosophical truths that

God is one, the soul is immortal, that the law of *karma* rules the universe, that the Self takes repeated births because of its karmas, and that salvation is our ultimate aim and that this aim can be attained.

The Bhagavadgita

If one likes to know the name of only one book that can give a knowledge of the basic philosophy of India, one can name the *Bhagavadgita.* Although, historically, it is a part of the *Mahabharata*, it has now an independent status solely because of its philosophical and religious aspect. Vyasa has rightly declared in the *Mahabharata* that if the Gita has been studied, one need not study any other scripture, because it has come right from the mouth of God.

The philosophy of the Gita can be summarized in the following words:

1. God is one. He has created the universe out of himself through his wonderful power, *Yoga-Maya.*
2. Everything that we see in the world is but a form of God.
3. Man is, really speaking, the Self, a form of God and, therefore, immortal and beyond every sorrow an agony.
4. Being the Self, one should not be swayed by one's passions and should try to go above them and become a *sthitaprajna* not affected by any loss or gain, victory or defeat, etc.
5. Man can regain his pristine spiritual glory through practice. There are the ways of knowledge, devotion, action and meditation. One may choose any path of his liking. However, the path of devotion is the best.
6. This universe is not an illusion. It is a battle ground of the right-minded and the wrong-minded persons. One should fight against the evil without caring for the outcome. It has to be noted that the ultimate victory belongs to the good, because God incarnates himself to save the world from being overpowered by the evil and to inspire the good to continue their fight.
7. One should never shun work. Even when a person has gained the ultimate knowledge, one should continue to work for the welfare of the world.
8. Nobody can give you salvation. Salvation has to be attained by a person himself through right thinking and right conduct.
9. The advice that salvation can be attained through selfless action

in whatever status you may be having in society is the cardinal feature of the Gita.

Vedic Religion

The Vedic religion has been known as *Sanatana* religion, i.e. eternal religion. And it is really so, because while most of other so-called religions are just sects, the Vedic religion has no limitation of any kind and description. It is neither restricted to any specific place, nor to any community, nor to any language, nor to any ritual, nor to any time. It is absolutely free from every restriction. Vedic religion (Hindu religion) does not need any priest or place or ritual for initiation. Any person who accepts that the Brahman is the only reality and the entire universe is His manifestation and the realization of one's real spiritual nature is possible by following a moral path is a follower of the Vedic religion.

The very term Dharma has been derived from the root "dhri" "meaning to support". Thus Dharma is that which is the supporting and sustaining principle of the universe and life. Man by nature is spirit. Dharma is that which sustains this spiritual nature. A person may worship the Real through worshiping an idol or by visiting a temple or by going on a pilgrimage or through certain traditional ritual. But this is just a beginning. Eventually, all this has to be left behind. Beginning can be made from anywhere. But the ultimate objective is to reach the Real. Swami Vivekananda has stated that it is good to be born in a church, but it is bad to die there. One should not and cannot put on the clothes that one wore in childhood even when one has grown up.

The very term Rama means the pervading principle of the universe. The term Krishna means that which attracts. Thus the terms Rama and Krishna mean the very Ultimate Reality that draws us because of its beauty. The *Bhagavata* states that Krishna is God.

Some people fail to understand the meanings of terms like *yajna*, *pashu-bali*, etc. *Yajna* simply means any act that propitiates God. It is not an act of sacrificing any animal. The term *Pashu Bali* means the sacrifice of one's animal tendency. The Vedic religion has its own language of symbols. When one tries to describe even the spiritual domain, one has to use the terms of this very world. But the meanings are definitely different. Just as science has its own symbolic language, religion too has its own language. A critical mind, not acquainted with this, fails to understand the meanings of religious language of the Vedic religion. This is why the *Mahabharata* states that the essence of religion is hidden in a cave *(dharmasya tatvam nihitam guhayam).* Religion is creative by its very nature. In India it has inspired art, literature and social thinking to rise to great heights. The great temples of the South, Khajuraho, Konark and Ellora and the caves of Ajanta, etc., prove this point.

It is worth noting that Dharma has not been divorced from philosophy in India. In the West generally religion and philosophy have not been mixed with the result that there religion is based on faith alone. In fact faith is another name of religion in the West. The result has not been happy in the West because this separation of religion and philosophy has inspired people to fight like brutes. European history tells us that a war lasting over a hundred years was waged in Europe between the Christians and the followers of Islam. Many persons were tortured in the name of religion. Such things did not happen in India due to a close association between religion and philosophy. Every philosopher in India is also a man of religion. This holds good in the case of Shankara, Ramanuja, Vallabha and every other philosophic thinker. Philosophy *(darshan)* means realization of the Truth through actual conduct. Ritualism is not religion. This has been declared by the *Bhagavadgita* itself. In real religion a person becomes a transformed soul. There is a complete harmony between knowledge, devotion and action in a religious person. Pilgrimage, fasting, idolworship and other similar acts can help in the inculcation of religious spirit. But soon a person goes much beyond them, just as one casts off a ladder after ascending to a higher destination. The distinctions of caste, creed, sex, sect, wealth all vanish. In the language of the *Bhagavadgita*, a religious person becomes dedicated to God from all aspects of personality, knowledge, devotion, action *(sarva-bhanena)*. And after realizing God, he becomes the universal being like God *(brahmavid bhramaiva bhavati)*.

This is really eternal religion. Eternal religion can be only that religion which is free from all restrictions and distinctions and which accepts eternal values like universal love, cooperation etc. Of course, a person can rise to that height only gradually and through a disciplined life alone. In short, it may be stated that religion, according to the Santana Dharma, consists in

> "Melting our limits in the illimitable
> Turning the finite into infinity."

Ethics: No British Gift

There are some who think that India had no ethics. They believe ethics came to India with the British. This kind of opinion only betrays ignorance of the fact that India had a highly developed ethical philosophy right from the beginning of the Vedic period. The *Rig Veda* tells us about the presence of Rita that rules the universe. "He is the custodian of the Rita, the binding Soul of the universe, the unity-in-difference in the cosmic and the moral order", states the Rig Veda. Gods are the guardians of the Moral Truth (*ritasya gopa*). Even the rivers flow because of this Rita.

But in India, ethics, philosophy, religion, science all were intermixed. It is just like our life in which thoughts, feelings, action, imagination all are intermixed. That is why some persons fail to see the presence of ethical philosophy in the ancient Indian literature. Still further, in India ethical philosophy has a metaphysical base. When Christian religion states that one should love one's neighbour or should care for one's neighbour's welfare, this statement has to be accepted on the foundation of faith alone; no reason for this advice has been provided. But when Lord Krishna states in the *Bhagavadgita* that a man should not make any difference while giving a cordial treatment between a learned Brahmin and animals like a cow, an elephant, or even a dog or an outcaste (V-18), the statement is based on the metaphysical position that the entire universe is nothing but a manifestation of God.

There is still another feature of Indian ethics. It is didactic and hortative. Thus in Indian ethics there are clear instructions like "One should not covet the wealth of others," "One should obey one's parents", "One should not tell a lie", etc. These instructions give a clear guidance to people. In the West, there are long discussions about theories like Hedonism, Perfectionism, Intuitionism, etc.. This theoretical discussion may be scholarly, but it gives little guidance in practising ethical philosophy.

It should be remembered that in India ethics has a spiritual aim before itself. Ethical conduct helps a man in moving in the direction of emancipation.

Literature concerning ethical philosophy is quite vast so far as ancient India is concerned. Right from the Vedas and the Upanishads to the *Dharma-shastra*, *Smritis* and *Puranas*, we have enormous literature concerning moral philosophy. But a very lucid analysis of ethical philosophy is found in the *Bhagavadgita*.

The *Gita* tells us, after giving an analysis of human nature, that no man can remain inactive. Man is so constituted that he has to do some kind of action either on physical or mental or on both levels. Hence, man has no option, so far as action is concerned. But it is up to him to act in a selfish manner or in an unselfish way. Our moral ideal should be to act in a selfless manner. The rationale for a selfless action too has been provided. If we analyse an act, we find five factors present there, viz. the substratum of act, the performer of the act, the instrument of the act, various efforts and chance factor. For example, suppose Mr. X wants to do some business. Suppose he tries to establish cloth business. Cloth business can be called the substratum. Mr X is, of course, its performer. Money to be invested is the instrument. Taking any shop in the market and keeping many types of cloth along with efficient salesmen and giving any advertisement, etc., are the efforts that he shall have too undertake. But despite all these efforts and investment, nobody can say from the beginning that he would certainly earn huge profits. It is a matter of chance that he may earn. There is a chance that he may lose.

According to the *Gita*, the first four factors are in the hands of a person; but the fifth factor is not. Hence, if a person gains, he should not assert that the success is entirely due to him and if he loses, he should not think that he has lost. The term used for chance is "daiva" which may mean the wish of God. Under the circumstances, the best thing is to act in a selfless manner. This type of acting has one advantage from the worldly point of view. A person shall concentrate solely on the way of his acting. Thus his acting will be more efficient than that of a person whose mind is fixed on the outcome alone. For example, a student who tries to pass an examination through unfair means is a case of inefficient acting.

The right type of student is that who studies diligently and appears in an examination sincerely without using any unfair means. There is still another reason. But it is metaphysical. According to the *Samkhya* system, the entire world is the result of an interplay of *Sattva, Rajas* and *Tamas*, the constituents of Prakriti, the Primary cause of creation. The Self is without any activity. He is simply a witness of the drama of the activities and movement going on in the world. What a person calls his action is thus simply the action of the three gunas, viz. *Sattva, Rajas* and *Tamas*. Why should the Self then think that he is acting?

Thus it has been proved by the *Gita* that selfless action alone is desirable. The ideal of the *Gita* is a man called *Sthita-prajna*, that is, a person who is not affected by the positive or negative results of an action. The *Gita* also advocates the ideal of acting for the welfare of all beings.

The *Gita* also gives us a list of *daivi gunas* or the virtues and the *asuri gunas* or the vices that are to be shunned. Chapter XVI contains the details. Fearlessness, purity of mind, a tendency to give charity to deserving persons, self-restraint, performance of good acts, study of the scriptures, austerity, non-violence, truthfulness, a spirit of self-sacrifice for the good of others, keeping anger under control, etc., are the virtues recommended by the *Gita*. Ego, pride, greed, sensuality, etc., are the vices that should be avoided.

People are classified by the *Gita*, on the basis of their temperaments, in four *varnas*, viz. Brahmin, Kshatriya, Vaishya and Shudra. But it has been explained that no *varna* is superior to any other varna. All varnas are equal. Nobody should try to imitate anybody else and should perform his duty in a selfless manner. It is the spirit in which an act is performed which is important. One should not shun one's duty despite any odd.

The *Gita* sets a unique ideal of conduct before us. The dignity of the individual has been given the importance it deserves; but at the same time it has been explained that the entire human community has to be accepted as the form of the great lord and, therefore, emancipation lies in acting for the welfare of one and all in a spirit of disinterested and dedicated being. Ethical philosophy is not a superstructure thrust on an individual; it is a process of evolution of an individual to realize his real personality. India has a high ethical philosophy that is still very relevant. In fact, more relevant to the modern atomic age where wars and conflicts can prove to be totally destructive.

7

RELEVANCE OF INDIAN CULTURE

WE HAVE studied the nature of Indian culture in the previous chapters. But a question may be asked "What is its utility in the modern period? We are living in a new world. How can the Indian culture discussed by us be relevant to the modern age of atomic weapons and the fastest means of communication"? An answer to this question has to be given.

As we know, culture is the moving force of mankind. It is as important to know "what we should become" as it is important to know what we actually are. A human being needs an ideal for evolution, for progress. Evolution is not a mechanical process, it is a rational process so far as human beings are concerned. As culture signifies the ideal to the height of which we have to rise, we must try to understand the best type of culture. The best type of culture is that which is the richest in both the extensive and intensive aspects.

By the extensive aspect is meant the area covered by the culture. Generally culture is restricted to a limited community. For example, there is German culture, English culture, French culture, etc. In all these cases, culture has a very limited field. This has to be contrasted with the extensive aspect of Indian culture. There is in fact no Indian culture because it is as extensive as the world itself. For Indian culture, the whole world is one family *(vasudhaiva kutumbakam)*. The *Atharva Veda* declares "The entire earth is my mother. I am the son of mother earth" *(mata bhumih, putro' ham prithivyah)*. For Indian culture man is, in fact, the immortal being. Everybody should realize that he is the immortal son of the immortal supreme Being.

shrinvantu vishve amritasy putras
aye dhamani divyani tasthuh

Manu states that the effort of every Indian should be to bring nobility in the mind of every person inhabiting any corner of our earth. The attitude of Indian culture is that there is no ground for discrimination between one man and another on the basis of nationality, because the entire earth is one, indivisible whole. Irrationality hidden in man is responsible for all the distinctions and differences that are found on the earth.

The reason for this universal outlook is to be found in its philosophy. If we consider culture to be an organism, philosophy is its soul, commerce and trade is its stomach, art and literature are its heart, knowledge is its head, polity is its arms, religion is its conduct. Thus philosophy is the moving force of any culture and as the Brahman is the ultimate reality, according to the Indian philosophy, there is no room for any restriction or limitation in outlook.

The *Rig Veda* expresses its universal outlook and concern for universal peace and amity in the following words:

"Let your thoughts be one and single.
Let your hearts be joined in one.
Both the mind at rest in unison
At peace with all.
So may be." *(Rig Veda* X 129.4)

Thus we find that Indian culture crosses the boundaries of nationalities, religion and geographical divisions. It believes in welfare of the entire world. Even the plants and mountains, not to talk about human beings alone, are the concern of Indian culture.

Now let us give our attention to be intensive aspect of culture. By intensive aspect is meant those qualities which are given supreme importance by culture. If we look to other cultures we find that every culture gives importance – supreme importance – to specific qualities like heroic qualities or artistic qualities. The Greek culture, for example, gave supreme importance to physical beauty. Emphasis on the physical aspect is even now an outstanding characteristics feature of the Western culture. In the modern scientific culture a tendency to give utmost importance to conquest over nature is evident. Everywhere in the west the new generation likes to pay every attention to conquering of external nature like the mountains, sea, air, planets, etc. The German thinkers like Nietzsche paid utmost importance to the conquest of nations resulting in the rise of Hitler. The USA seems to give utmost importance to wealth and opulence. These concepts of culture have their own beauty and importance. But they are mundane in nature. That is why Indian culture without ignoring the importance of physical things gave higher importance to spiritual factors. In this context, the following words of the *Bhagavadgita* are worth noting because they disparage an earthly attitude:

> "Possessed of hypocrisy, conceit and arrogance and given to insatiable passion, and adopting false doctrines due to delusion, they take to action with impure vows. Giving themselves over to endless cares terminating only with death, and given to the enjoyment of sensuous pleasures, they believe the highest limit of joy to consist only in this. . . . Self-important, unbending, filled with the intoxication of wealth and honour, performing nominal sacrifice for show in a lawless manner." (XVI 10-21)

Such persons are not appreciated by the *Gita*. They are persons of *Asuri gunas*. Thus, the Indian culture gives inferior status to worldly qualities as compared with spiritual qualities.

The Unifying Force

Spiritual qualities are always unifying, synthetic and constructive in nature. They result in a conduct that is positively creative and never gives birth to fissiparous tendencies. According to the *Bhagavadgita* (XV. 1-2), the universe is like the *peepal* tree. Its roots lie in the Primal Being; its stem is represented by the creator; its leaves are the Vedas; its branches are the different species of the living beings; it is nourished by the three *Gunas*, viz. *Sattva, Rajas* and *Tamas*; its tender leaves are sense enjoyment. Therefore, all those qualities are desirable which do justice to the unifying character of the world.

The history of the world is a history of an endless series of wars and conflicts. The situation has worsened in the modern age. W.B. Yeats has depicted the situation in the following words:

> "Things fall apart: the centre cannot hold,
> Mere anarchy is loosed upon the world,
> The blood-dimmed tide is loosed, and everywhere
> The ceremony of innocence is drowned;
> The best lack all conviction, while the worst
> are full of passionate intensity."

In this Atomic Age, any war means total destruction of mankind.

Therefore, we certainly need right type of men, who can understand the gravity of the situation and can avoid the situation of conflict and confrontation. American poet Oliver Wendel Holms has rightly written:

> "God give us men – a time
> like this demands
> Great hearts, strong minds
> true faith and willing hands;
> Men, whom the lust of office
> will not buy,
> Men, who have opinion
> and a will,
> Men, who have honour,
> Who will not lie."

This can be possible only by accepting "Indian" culture. It is rich from the standpoints of art, literature, religion, ethics, polity, social philosophy and even science. But all these have drawn inspiration from its basic philosophy of unity of life. The ultimate values are never forgotten. This is clear from the statement of Maitreyi that she was interested only in that which could bestow immortality on her. Aurobindo has described the correct nature of Indian culture by stating, "A true happiness in this world is the right terrestrial aim of man, and true happiness lies in finding and maintenance of a natural harmony of spirit, mind and body. A culture is to be valued to the extent to which it has discovered the right key of this harmony and organised its expressive motives and movements," and adding that Indian culture answers these demands in ample measure. It has an excellence that cannot be denied.

One should not think that Indian culture does not give due importance to the world. The fact is that according to Indian culture it is our duty to establish a reign of peace, prosperity and amity in this very world, because God attaches so much importance to this world that He Himself takes birth on earth when the latter is threatened by the destructive activities of the evil-doers, and sets things right. Therefore, to save the world from catastrophe and destruction is the pious duty of every son of this mother earth. Our art, literature, science, everything should be dedicated to the welfare of one and all. Indian culture is a ladder that helps a man to rise to the sky of doing good to all.

Indian culture is the real culture because one cannot imagine any limitation of blind nationalism or religious sectarian outlook in culture. But if we are asked to describe the significance of Indian culture in the context of other "cultures", we can say that it is "queen supreme of all the host of queens", because for every nation its culture is the "queen". If some persons fail to understand the beauty of Indian culture, it is not due to any imagined fact that it has no beauty, but it is only because of the fact that in the words of Kalidasa "folk have different tastes".

We can state that Indian culture is ruled by three basic concepts, viz. *Dharma, Yoga* and *Yajna.* The implied meaning of Dharma is faith in a universal law that sustains the universe and with which a direct link has to be established by an individual through understanding and actual conduct. Religion was never accepted in the sense of any sect in India. As *Dharma* has been considered to be a sustaining and controlling principle of life, a person who follows it attains worldly prosperity *(abhyudaya)* as well as liberation *(nihshreyas).* That is, a person and a society pursuing the path of *Dharma* prosper both temporally and spiritually. A life of *Dharma* can be possible only if one gets a vision of the Supreme (the *Brahman)* where harmony – an integral harmony – prevails. The *Bhagavadgita* declares,

> "That by which man sees one imperishable entity in all beings undivided among the divided, know that knowledge to be *Sattvika.*" (XVIII 20)
>
> "That intelligence which knows what is a right action and what is a wrong action, what should be done and what ought not to be done, what is fear and what constitutes fearlessness, what is bondage and what is liberation, that alone is *Sattvika.*" (XVIII 30)

Thus *Dharma* gives an integral view of life and the universe. That is why it constitutes the first supreme end *(purushartha)* of life. Yoga stands for a right view about action. One's right attitude towards life must be reflected in one's conduct. Any conduct inspired by an integral view of life is called *Yoga.* That is why the *Gita* describes *Yoga* as dexterity in action *(yogah karmasu kaushalam).* If an action is prompted by animal urges like rage, delusion, ignorance, etc., it is not *Yoga.* Only selfless action constitutes *Yoga* because such an act does not generate any bad result. When one develops a *Yogic* attitude in life, one indulges in those acts which contribute to the welfare of others. Any act that aims at the well-being of one and all is called a sacrifice

(Yajna). The *Gita* declares, "Man is bound by shackles of *Karma* only when engaged in actions other than work performed for the sake of sacrifice". (III 9)

The spirit of an act that has assumed the status of a *Yajna* is to provide food even to insects . . ., not to talk about men, animals and other beings.

If our modern world too gets an inspiration from the factors of Dharma, Yoga and *Yajna*, it will see a rise of the real culture which shall benefit one and all. Culture cannot gain its true nature unless it is imbued in spirituality. Indian culture in its ideal form presents an inspiring ideal for all those imperfect notions of culture which aspire to gain perfection and maturity. One must transcend one's animal nature to get a vision of the real culture as envisaged by Indian thinkers.

It should be remembered that the real culture demands a radical change in the outlook of a man. He must think that he is not a person encaged in the limits of any creed, sex, colour or nationality. He must realize in his heart of heart

"I am the son of earth; earth is my mother"
(mata bhumih putro' ham prithivyah)

Culture implies liberation of a person from all those shackles that limit his illimitable personality in any way. This is the studied opinion of Indian seers.

8

PSYCHOLOGY IN INDIA

THIS IS not the place to give a detailed account or a complete picture of Indian psychology. But some brief survey of Indian psychology is both necessary and desirable in view of the fact that in the absence of such an attempt we shall not be able to form a complete view of the distinct approach of India towards psychology.

It is evident that a study of psychology in the modern sense of the term was not attempted in the old India. And yet it will have to be accepted that the Indians of the past were able to search out something quite valuable in the domain of human psychology. Even the Vedic seers who were primarily interested in religion and philosophy tried at times to study the human being himself. From the point of view of psychology the *Yajur-Veda-Samhita* has divided human being in the following parts: head *(si-rah)*, face *(mukham)*, hair of the head *(keshah)*, facial hair *(smashru)*, breath *(prana)*, eyes *(chakshu)*, hearing apparatus *(shrotram)*, tongue *(jihva)*, speech *(vak)*, mind *(manas)*, fingers *(angulih)*, arms *(bahu)*, hands *(hastau)*, ears *(karnau)*, soul *(atma)*, breast *(urah)*, vertebrae *(prishtih)*, belly *(udara)*, neck *(griva)*, buttocks *(shroni)*, thighs *(uru)*, knees *(januni)*, legs *(janghe)*, foot *(pad)*, navel *(nabhi)*, anus *(payu)*, testicles *(andau)*, nails *(lomani)*, skin *(tvac)*, muscle *(mamsa)*, bone *(asthi)*, marrow *(majja)*. (*The Vedic Index*, p. 361) (*Rig Veda* 10, 163.3)

The poets of the *Rig Veda* knew that it was the heart (hrit) that was involved in the psychological experiences. They speak of "the pangs of grief in the heart" (RV 10.103.2, *hritsu shokaih*), "holding fear in the heart". (RV 10.84.7 *bhiyam dadhana hridayeshu*)

This heart is distinguished from mind *(manas)* since it is the heart that experiences longing (RV 1.123.6), grief (RV. 10.103.12) or pleasures (RV. 1.43.1)

Mind is an instrument of reason or rationality. Its function is compared to the winnowing of barley through the sieve (RV 10.10.6). Mind is the faculty that" investigates and considers" (RV 10.7.5, *manasa vimrishta*).

That the heart and mind are different was very clearly realised by the seers of the *Rig Veda* as is clear from their prayer

"May our resolutions be uniform
and our hearts united;
May our minds be one,
That we live well together."

(Samani va akutih, samana hridayani vah;
samanam astu vo mano, yatha vas susaha sati) (10.191.4)

In the well-known *Nasadiya Sukta* of the *Rig Veda* we find a clear recognition of a third important factor of psychology too. The poet observes in the hymn: darkness was hidden in the womb of darkness and everywhere was the watery mass, but then there sprang *kama* which was the primeval germ of mind. Schopenhauer and Deussen have taken the term in the sense of will. Of course the will meant here is not a personal will but the unscrutable will that is the moving power of this universe. However this implies that the seers of the *Rig Veda* did realise to an extent the importance of will as well, because what is true of the Supreme is also true to some extent for the individual. Thus all the three important elements of human mind, viz. cognition, feeling and will are accepted in the form of manas, hridaya and kama respectively. It is really creditable for the thinkers of the Rig Veda that they could understand the significance of these three elements even in the distant past of humanity.

In the Upanishads again we find that an attempt has been made to understand a human being even in a psychological manner. The *Brihadaranyaka Upanishad* contains a dialogue between Janaka and Yajnavalkya. The King Janaka questions and sage Yajnavalkya answers:

"What serves man for light?" "Sun".
"When the sun has set?" Moon".
"When the moon also has set?" "Fire".
"When the fire has gone out?" "Speech".
"When the speech is hushed?" "One's own consciousness". (Brih *adaranyaka* 4.3.1f)

This account makes it clear that the Upanishads held that

consciousness is the distinguishing feature of human beings.

The *Aitareya Upanishad* goes still further and declares that intelligence is essentially a man's attribute (3.5.3). But perhaps a still more revealing is the account of personality furnished by the Upanishads. According to the Upanishadic opinion human personality has five levels, beginning from the gross one to the sublime one. The first one is *annamaya kosha* and is the physical basis of the person's functions; the next level is *prana-maya kosha* or the level of sensations; *manomaya kosha*, which comes next, represents the transition from the physical to the abstract: this stage is marked by the rise of perceptual processes and ideation. The dimension of consciousness, *vijnana* follows the *manomaya kosha*. Finally comes the *anandamaya kosha* or the dimension of bliss. This is the highest stage of human life according to the *Chhandogya Upanishad*.

We come across an interesting story in the Upanishads which has been described as the "War of Senses" (*Chhandogya*, 5.1 6-12; *Brihadaranyaka* 6.1.7-13; *Kaushituki* 2.14) wherein it has been established in an allegorical manner that the various senses, viz. the eyes, the ears, the speech, the mind are capable of fulfilling their functions only because of consciousness. They all are merely the emanations of consciousness.

"Once the senses started quarreling among themselves, each asserting its own superiority, saying 'I am superior'. Then they approached their father Prajapati, and asked: 'Sir, which of us is most superior?' He replied: That one without which the body is worst off is the most superior among you'. Speech then left the body and went away. He remained away for a year and on returning was surprised to see that the body continued as it used to be, if only as dumb. Then the eyes went off, then the ears and then the mind, but when they returned they found that the body continued, if only as blind, as deaf or as a simpleton. It was now the *prana's* turn to go off, but when it attempted to go they all cried: 'Do not go. Remain, you are most superior'. For as "a fine horse would pull out the very pegs to which it is tied, *prana* pulled out the other senses." How suggestive is this allegory.

According to the *Aitareya-aranyaka* (2.4.3.6), mind implies "that faculty in an organised body which thinks". Consciousness or waking condition *(jagriti)* was considered to be "the condition of being in this world" (Br. Up. 4.3.9); dreaming was thought to be a condition "which is neither alive nor dead" *(Atharva Veda* 6.46.1). The description of dreaming is very suggestive. "There are really no objects (in the dream); but the dreamer projects them from himself. . . . He is a creator. . . . As a great fish moves along both the banks of the stream, even so the dreamer moves along the two conditions: sleeping and waking." (Br. Up. 4.3.9-18) The modern psychoanalysis shall hail this statement of the Upanishads as quite true: He who desires, dreams; he who does not desire does not dream. (Br. Up. 3.3.19).

The Upanishads also talk about a dreamless sleep *(Sushupti)*. "Even as an eagle, having flown in the air, gets tired, folds its wings and descends to its nest, even so an individual fatigued from the waking life falls asleep." (Br. Up. 43.19)

Even a list of mentations is provided by the *Aiteraya Upanishad*: consciousness *(samjnana)*, perception *(jnanan)*, discrimination *(vijnana)*, intelligence *(prajnana)*, wisdom *(medha)*, insight *(drishti)*, perseverance *(dhriti)*, thought *(mati)*, impulse *(juti)*, memory *(smriti)*, conception *(samkalpa)*, purpose *(kratu)* desire *(kama)*, and will *(vasha)* (3.5.1).

Oldest System of Thought

The *Samkhya* system is perhaps the oldest system of thought in India. Many of its concepts have been accepted by almost all the systems, notably by the *Vedanta* system. The most important concept of the *Samkhya* is "purusha" or self or "the principle behind consciousness". Writing on the *Samkhya*, Dr. Radhakrishnan says: "it is postulated as an element in our personality to illumine the mental processes, which are the outcome of the physical organisation".[1] According to the *Samkhya* there is a plurality of the "purushas". They are thus empirical individuals and not a transcendental reality of the *Vedanta*.

The *Samkhya* postulates three principles of Prakriti or nature, viz. *Sattva, Rajas* and *Tamas*. *Sattva* represents knowing, *Rajas* represents feeling and *Tamas* represents willing aspects of the self. The self is able to act because of the trinity of these principles. This account about the human consciousness is true even from the point of view of modern psychology. The term "guna", which has been used to denote the three aspects, means "capacity" or potentiality. Thus the three tendencies are quite basic to human nature.

The *Bhagvadgita* has very rightly pointed out the three types of personality, viz. *Sattvika, Rajasa* and *Tamasa*. A person of *sattvika* dimension is one in whom knowledge predominates; a person of *Rajas* dimension is one in whom feeling or emotions dominate; and a person of *Tamas* dimension is one in whom impulsive conduct is the dominating factor.

In the Buddhist system we find that body *(rupa)*, mind *(citta)* and mental states *(chetasika)* have been described as the essential factors of the individual and his behaviour *(Abhidammatthasangaha* 1, 2). The theory of *Samghata* of the Buddhists comes very near the Gestalt psychology, as it is "a gestalting factor with an action-orientation" (*Majjhima Nikaya* 2,32). Every act of perception consists of two stages, viz. sensory organisation and psychological organisation by "labelling" *(adhivachana)* according to Mrs. Rhys Davids.

The Pali Atthasalini explains in great detail the various processes involved in the perceptual act. Four phases are mentioned: sense-stimulation; assimilation; apprehension of the sign; and comprehension of meaning.

The problems of perception and illusion have been given very elaborative treatments in different systems of India. Kumarila, Prabhakara, Sautrantika schools of the Buddhists, Madhva, Ramanuja all have their own peculiar theories to offer to explain the phenomenon of illusion.

It may be found interesting to note in passing the theory of illusion as held by Ramanuja. Illusion is not an unreal or invalid cognition according to him; insofar as it points to an objective presence, it is real, and insofar as it points to some features similar to a real thing, it is valid. For example, when one mistakes shell for silver, there is something real about the glistening, whiteness, etc. found in a shell that make it possible to mistake it for silver. There is neither a defect in the sense organ, nor can it be attributed to any imagination.

The theories of *anyathakhyati*, i.e., a theory that illusion is a phenomenon where the object is apprehended as differently by the actively participating agent, wherein the presence of an objective ground *(adhisthana)* and erroneous ascription (aropa) of a recollected idea are essential; the theory of *Akhyativada* or Imperception Argument holding that the error in perception is due to omission occasioned by confusion in memory (*smritipramosha*; the theory of *Atmakhyati* emphasising the role of subjective projection or externalisation of an idea not permissible by practical utility; the theory of *Asatkhyati* or Objectless Perception according to which illusions are figures without ground as the silver that is seen in a shell is a figure brought out from the void and possesses an unnatural externality; the theory of *Anyathakhyati* of Madhva, according to which an illusion is based on reality and consists in the misinterpretation of sensory data, may be mentioned here to give an idea as to the extent the problems of perception and illusion have been tackled.

Some account of Indian psychology can also be gleaned from the works of Sanskrit criticism like Bharata's *Natya-shastra*, Jagannatha's *Rasagangadhara,* and the works by Rajashekhara, Rudrata, Bhamaha, Vagbhata, Dandin and Anandavardhana.

From the point of view of psychology, Bharata's theory of *Rasa* or relish is the most outstanding. *Rasa* or aesthetic delight is the secret of success of any writer. It is produced due to the emotive situation in human setting, consisting of the physical cause of the basic mental state *(vibhava)*, the mimetic changes, which are inspired by the aroused basic mental state and as such are indicative of internal state *(anubhava)*, and the transient emotions *(vyabhichari-bhava)*. The basic mental state is the most important phase of this configuration and the basic mental state is the aesthetic delight *(sthayi bhavo rasah smritah)*.

The eight basic rasas or dominant tendencies are: love, laughter, sorrow, anger, energy, fear, repulsion and wonder and can be compared with the list of instincts submitted by McDougall.

Indian Psychology aimed at Spirituality

It was never the intention of the writer to deal with the nature of psychology of India in detail here. He intended merely to suggest that Indian literature contains some significant material which throws a flood of light on the human psychology as understood in India. The above account, it is presumed, must have given the readers a glimpse about the psychological material present in India. In the end it may be added that besides the works on philosophy, religion, and literature, even the books on medicine or Ayurveda contain a lot of material shedding light on the Indian concept of psychology. But the sole object of Indian treatment of the subject was to sublimate the individual from the gross level to the spiritual one in a most enlightened way. The Indians knew the principle of psychology leading to spirituality as shall be clear from the following sloka of the *Bhagvadgita*:

> "Sense objects cease for him, who does not enjoy them with his senses; but the taste for them persists. this relish also disappears in the case of the man of stable mind when he sees the supreme." (II-59)

NOTE

1. "The Sankhya System", *The Philosophical Quarterly*, 1927, 2, 4, p.266.

9

RELIGIOUS PHILOSOPHY OF KALIDASA

DHARMA, WHICH has been popularly translated as religion, occupies a significant position in Indian culture. Indeed it has been accepted that religion alone can lead a person to the portals of progress and perfection. Even Indian philosophy aims at giving correct guidance in the domain of religion because mere speculations about the ultimate Truth are not sufficient. They must be aimed at the realization of practical solutions of the problems of pain and unhappiness which burden our day-to-day life. Religion aims at a qualitative transformation of human conduct, because this is the only way of making one's life free from the traces of worldly miseries an misfortunes.

Kalidasa was not only a great poet and dramatist of India, he was well-versed in the philosophy, religion, Vedic lore, etc. Though the main aim of Kalidasa was to depict human emotions and sentiments, he did try to express his religious philosophy whenever he could find an occasion to do so. We should not forget that Kalidasa had his own views about religion. Of course, these views emerged due to the influence of the lofty philosophical teaching of the Upanishads and the Puranas, but they belonged to Kalidasa as he accepted them after thoughtful consideration and give them an expression in his own unique manner. Moreover, only a foolish person is led by the opinion of others.

The religious scene of India at the time of Kalidasa was not very heartening. Two powerful anti-Vedic thoughts in the form of Jainism and Buddhism had become strong. These anti-Vedic thoughts gained strength as they were accorded royal patronage and the people tried to follow that religion which was accepted by their king. Specially, Buddhism became very dominant, because it attacked casteism and the violence associated with the sacrifices. An additional factor that helped Buddhism in swelling the number of its adherents was the rich donation it received from the rich and influential sections of society which enabled the Buddhistic *Viharas* to become asylums of easy and comfortable life. Who does not like an easy-going and respectful life? Hence, people accepted Buddhism in thousands. The Brahmans who accepted Buddhism also tried to prepare profound commentaries of Buddhistic teachings.

Hindu religion itself had at least two important sects of *Vaishnavism* and *Shaivism*. Even if these sects did not quarrel openly, there existed a thin but perceptible line of disagreement between them. It is queer that the land of the Upanishadic thought had become flooded with currents of religious disharmony and disagreements. While it cannot be established that God created men, it can be proved beyond any shadow of doubt that man does create God. Hindu religion demonstrates this very fact by accepting the principle of a favourite god or *ishta devata*. If every person does not create any god, at least he selects a god for himself from among the, wide variety offered to him. This selection implies that a person is free to accept a particular type of deity. It is a remarkable feat of the Indian mind that out of this wide variety of deities, the cult of the Vedanta or non-dualism was created. Kalidasa did not decry the different concepts of god, because he knew that people possess different and divergent likings or aptitudes. So far as Kalidasa was concerned, he liked to worship Lord Shiva. Shiva attracted Kalidasa's heart that was filled with art and beauty. That is why Kalidasa invoked Shiva at the beginning of his plays. For example, he prays Shiva in the following words in the prologue to *Malvikagnimitra*:

> "Though occupying the position of undivided sovereignty over the whole universe – a position which is fruitful of several blessings to the humble and the devout – he is himself clad in elephant's skin; although his body is integrated with that of his beloved spouse into one single whole, he stands far above the self-restrained ascetics in the matter of keeping the mind completely aloof from sensual desires; though sustaining the entire creation with his eight forms, he has not a trace of pride in him. May that Lord dispel the element of darkness from your nature so that you may perceive the right path in the light of pure knowledge."

But no, it will be wrong to presume that Kalidasa was a blind ollower of the Shiva sect. When he prays in *Shakuntala*, "May the elf-existent, purple-throated God, whose power pervades everywhere, release me from the interminable chain of birth and death," he does not mean that his Lord is a petty god.

Kalidasa makes it clear in *Kumarasambhava* (canto VI) that his Shiva is the supreme God who is the author of the creation, preservation and dissolution of the universe, and who governs the creatures internally. In the second canto Brahma states: "That God is the self-luminous Supreme Spirit itself that abides permanently beyond all darkness and is outside all illusive appearances. The extent of his power can neither be measured by me nor by Vishnu."

For Kalidasa there is no distinction between Shiva and Vishnu. In *Kumarasambhava* he writes: "Manifesting thy exalted power through three successive states of thine existence, O Lord, thou alone art the cause of creation, preservation and destruction." In the *Raghuvamsha* he states:

> "Salutation to Thee, O Lord, who abidest in three different forms – being at first the creator of the universe, afterwards the upholder of it, and lastly the destroyer of it."

What is implied through these descriptions is that the Supreme God is one although sometimes he is thought to be Shiva and sometimes Vishnu.

Only One Supreme God

This point is made amply clear in *Kumarasambhava*:

> "It is essentially the same Being who splits itself into three different deities (for the performances of three different functions of creation, protection and destruction of the universe), each of whom is prior or posterior to the others by turns. Sometimes Shiva precedes Vishnu, sometimes Vishnu precedes Shiva, sometimes Brahma precedes either of the two, and they both precede him."

For Kalidasa Rama, Vishnu, Shiva, Brahma all are essentially one, viz. Supreme God *(Purusham Puratanam)*. It is in fact the imperceptible truth *(avyakto)*, one appearing in manifold forms *(sarvarupa-bhak)*. It is the same Truth which the yogis seek for liberation. Nobody can know its real nature It is, really speaking, beyond the reach of speech and mind.

In one word we can say that it is the Brahman of the Upanishads. Who can find out the secret of God the Supreme? Kalidasa seems to accept the authority of the Vedas with faith. Undue argumentation shall lead us nowhere. As the aptitudes and likings of people differ, one supreme Truth is understood in different forms and ways. But Kalidasa is of the firm opinion that all the paths leading to the Supreme are worthwhile. They all lead to Him as all the rivers meet in the ocean. Hence what is needed is a real understanding of the Truth and the consequent tolerance towards other seekers of the Truth.

What should be remembered is the fact that even the Supreme incarnates in the form of Rama, etc., for the protection of piety.

Kalidasa appears to favour the path of devotion as compared to the path of asceticism favoured by Jainism and Buddhism. Kalidasa states that body should not be neglected as it is an instrument of religious attainment. One cannot get freedom from desires through ascetic means, because they cannot be curbed in this way.

Similarly, he condemns renunciation of action. One should not abandon one's duties. Even God accepts incarnations to favour this smooth working of the world.

Kalidasa thus accepts the basic teaching of the Bhagavadgita and has indirectly condemned intolerance, asceticism and other worldliness prevalent at his time. He has reaffirmed the basic philosophy of the Upanishads and preached the acceptance of one's duties coupled with a sense of devotion. He gives due importance even to the religious celebrations because by nature man likes celebrations.

Kalidasa has thus advocated a sensible and feasible religious philosophy that can be acceptable even to a person of an average intelligence.

Our religion should so equip us that the temptations of the world shall not overwhelm us, even though we continue to live our worldly life and it should inspire us not to flee from it by adopting a negative attitude towards it. Kalidasa emphasizes this fact.

10

INDIAN CONCEPT OF EDUCATION FOR RULERS

IT IS evident that from the very beginning human wisdom endeavoured to shape the conduct of the rulers in the desirable direction by educating them in the right manner. Of course, the concept of education is likely to change in accordance with the changed times. But even though the change of time has seen certain prominent changes in the pattern of education meant for the royal persons or rulers, yet it should not be forgotten that despite the changes in the content of the educational pattern, certain factors were permanent, certain elements were of such character that no change came into their basic nature.

The *Rig Veda* which can be called the fountainhead of Indian culture, had a special adoration for Saraswati, the Goddess of learning. Sang the seer of the *Rig Veda*:

> "Saraswati causes to manifest the vast ocean of knowledge with which She illuminates the intellectual activities of all."
>
> *(Maho arnah Sarasvati*
> *pra cetayati ketuna;*
> *dhiyo vishva vi rajati.)* (1.3.12)

He uttered the innermost desire of his heart by praying: "Indeed the luminous rays of knowledge desirous to attain the Eternal Law feed full the world like the kine with udders ever replete with nourishing milk and as the rivers breaking asunder the mountain and flowing from its vicinity hasten towards the ocean from a distance; similarly you should do good to the world ever intending to acquire noble thoughts."

(Ritasya hi dhenavo vavashanah, smadughnih pipayanta

dyubhaktah paravatah sumatim bhikshamana vi sindhavah samaya sasruradrim.)

(*Rvg* 1.73.6)

On another occasion the seer addresses the Lord of Speech, Brihaspati:

"O Brihaspati, the original source of the earliest speech which is the most excellent and spotless and which the learned men pronounce by giving name (to all existing objects) remains treasured within the cave-like heart (of the wise), the very same becomes manifest by (their force) of love."
(Brihaspate prathamam vaco agram, yatprairata namadheyam dadhanah yadesham shreshtham yadaripramasit, prena tadesham nihitam guhavih.)

(*Rvg* 10.71.1)

It was not meant that this learning should be confined only to the Brahmins. It was meant for one and all including of course the ruling class.

"O mankind, as I address this propitious speech of mine (i.e. the Vedas) to all the people, i.e. to Brahmanas (men devoted to the propagation of Divine knowledge), to Kshatriyas (men engaged in the ruling and administrating society), to Shudras (men engaged in the manual work), and to Vaishyas (men engaged in trade and commerce) to those who are my own devotees and to them who are men of low dignity; May I be beloved to the learned and beloved to those who are bounteous in this world, may this object of mine be fulfilled and may this aim of mine be realized."

(yathemam vacam kalyanimavadanijanebhyah
brahmarajanyabhyam shudraya
caryyaya ca svaya caranaya;
priyo devanam dakshinayai
daturiha bhuyasamayam me kamah
samriddhyatamupa mado namatu.)

(Yajur Veda 26.2)

They were of the opinion that

"Truth, mighty eternal law, heroism, fitness, activity,

> knowledge of revelation, and self-sacrificing acts uphold the earth."
> *(satyam brihadriamugram diksha tapo, brahma yajnah prithivim dharayanti.)*
>
> *(Atharva Veda* 12.1.1)

They appreciated liberality, for they were of the firm opinion,

> "Surely all these wonderful objects of the world belong to such persons who are of charitable disposition; even the sun and the stars shine in the heaven for the liberal minded."
>
> *(dakshinavatamidimani citra*
> *dakshinavatam divi suryasah.)* (RV 1.125.6)

They aspired to have noble intentions (*shivasamkalpamastu*, YV 34-6) and desired to be devoid of any fear whatsoever:

> "May we be fearless of our friends and even of those who are unfriendly to us, may we never fall in dread of those whom we know and even of those whom we do not know; May we remain free from any apprehension by night and in the daytime, and may all the (beings residing in various) quarters be friendly to us."
> *(abhayam mitradabhayamatradabhayam jnatadabhayam paroksyata abhayam naktamabhayam diva nah, sarva asha mama mitram bhavantu.)*
>
> (AV 19.15.6)

They prayed that they should always be engaged in performing self-sacrificing acts (anyuryajnena kalpatam) and still further wrapped in enlightened spirit (*Yajur Veda* 9.21).

They wanted to become non-covetous and enjoy life in a spirit of non-attachment (*tena tyaktena bhunjitha*, YV 40.1). They preached the gospel of universal harmony in their social organization.

> "O ye mankind, let your object of life be one and the same; let your hearts be equal (in feeling) and let your minds be united together so that there may be an excellent common status of life for all."

> *(samani va akuthi, samana hridayani-vah:*
> *samanamastu vo mano yatha vah susahasati.)* (RV 10.191.4)

And, therefore, naturally they taught the ruler to be dutiful.

> "O ye organizers of human society, let the Brahmana devote himself to the propagation of divine knowledge, the governmental authority to the protection of people from distress."
> *(brahmane brahmanam kshatraya rajanyam.)*
> (YV 30.5)

We find in this manner that the Vedic seers taught the rulers to be the sincere servants of society, to sacrifice themselves at the altar of human welfare. There was no trace of narrowness in the teaching. Deceipt and falsehood were never taught to the rulers. What was taught was a lesson of universal sympathy, straight forward conduct, a spirit of sacrifice, and a cult of fearlessness. Deceipt is essentially a sign of weakness and timidness. We play cheating games with a person who excites fear in us. When we are not afraid, when we have no trace of selfishness, how can we be deceitful?

The Teaching of the Mahabharata

The *Mahabharata* has wielded immense influence upon the thought and conduct of Indian people. It contains an account of the teaching that must be given to the rulers. In the *Shanti Parva*, Bhishma expresses in unmistakable words the fact that truthfulness alone should be the policy of the ruler.

> "Nothing except truthfulness brings success to kings. Adopt straight-forwardness in all actions."
> *(na hi satyadrte kimcitd rajnam vai siddhikarakamarjavam sarvakaryeshvashrayetha kurunandana)*

> "A king following righteousness must always stand for whatever is good for the world, renouncing what is pleasant to himself."
> *(vartitavyam kurukshreshtha, sada dharmanuvartina*
> *svam priyam parityajya, yadyaldokshitam bhavet:)*

"That king is the best king in whose country, the people move about without fear, like sons in their father's house."
(Putra iva piturgehe vishaye yasya manavah
Nirbhaya vicarishyanti sa raja rajasattamah)

"His own self must be conquered by the king for all time; then only are his enemies to be conquered. Adopting virtue and material good, he should avoid passion and anger."
(Atma jeyassada rajna tato jeyashca shatravah
Dharmarthau pratigrihaniyat kamakrodhau ca varjayet)

"Harassing the subjects in his ignorance by taxes not found in the texts, and motivated by Artha alone, the king does harm to himself."
(Arthamulo'pi himsa ca kurute svayamatmanah
Karairashastradirishtairhi mohatsampidayanprajah)

"The ruler should always make arrangement for the security and maintenance of the poor, the helpless, the old and widowed women."
(Kripananathayriddhanam vidhavanam ca yoshitam
Yogakshemam ca vrittim ca nityameva prakalpayet)

"Let there be no beggars and no thieves in your kingdom."
(ma te rashtre yacaka bhaveyurma ca dasyavah)

"I think that the eye of the weak, of the sage and of the serpent is most unbearable; therefore, do not assail the weak."
(Durbalasya ca yaccakshur munerashivishasya ca
Avishamyatamam manye ma sma durbalamasadah)

"Son, consider that the powerless must never be insulted; let not the eyes of the weak burn you and your kinsmen. If one insulted, beaten or harassed, does not get his saviour, in that kingdom, divine punishment kills the ruler. My son, remaining in power, don't you live upon the powerless people. The tears that fall from those who weep, being falsely accused, kill the sons and cattle of those who make the false accusation."
(Durbalamstata manyetha nityamevavimanitan
Ma tvam durbalacakshunshi pradaheyussabandhvam

Vimanito hatah krushtastrataram cennavindati
Amanushakritastatra dando hanti naradhipam.

ma sma tata balasthatvam bhunjitha durbalam janam.
yani mithyabhishstanam patantyashruni rodatam
tani putranpashunghnanti tesham mithyabhishamsinam.)

"A king should build up his victory by means other than war: victory through war is said to be the worst."
(ayuddhenaiva vijayam vardhayedvasudhadhipah
jaghanyamahurvijayam yuddhena ca naradhipa.)

"Death through Dharma is better than victory through a sinful act."
(dharmena nidhanam shreyo na jayah papakarmana.)

"King, hear that which forms the basis of sins. Avarice, that huge rapacious animal (is the basis of sin); it is from avarice that sin proceeds; from it proceed sin, unrighteousness and worst misery; this is the root cause of fraud; everything proceeds from avarice. By the self-possessed person, this avarice, along with delusion, has to be conquered."
(Papasya yadadhishthanam tacchunushva naradhipa.
eko lobho mahagraho lobhatpapam pravartate.
atah papamadharmashca tatha duhkhmanuttamam.
nikritya mulametaddhi sarvam lobhatpravartate.
sa lobjassaha mohena vijetavyo jitatmana.)

Here we find an eternal message of righteousness for the rulers. War is not the desirable way of life. An attitude free from avarice, and marked by truthfulness should characterize the conduct of the rulers.

The *Mahabharata* has proclaimed that the rulers should be subservient to the Brahmanas. Here it is not meant by the *Mahabharata* to convey that a particular social class, a priest class, should dominate the government. What is meant is that the government must draw due guidance from the pious, from the people who love righteousness above anything else.

The Smritis

Hindu culture draws its inspiration from the Smriti literature. Hindu religion is said to be constituted by the Vedic, *Smriti* and Puranic literatures. The worldly conduct of the Hindus has been specially determined by the *Smriti* literature of India. It would, therefore, be useful to study what the Smritis state about rulers.

According to the *Yajnavalkya Smriti*, the ruler must belong to a morally elevated family *(kulina)*, with an ideal that is not abstract *(sthulalakshyah)*, grateful *(kritajna)*, respector of the aged *(vriddhasevaka)*, modest *(vinita)*, full of might *(satvasampanna)*, truthful *(satyavak)* and pious *(shuci)*. He should be able to take quick decisions *(adirghasutra)*, devoid of meanness (*ashudra*), prudent *(prajna)*, courageous *(shura)* (verses 309-312). The ruler must protect the subjects from the thieves and the exploiters (verse 336). He should be devoid of the traces of anger and avarice (verse 1, *Vyavaharadhyaya*).

The *Gautama Smriti* states that the ruler should be of righteous conduct *(sadhukari* and *sadhuvadi*), and equal to all *(samah prajasu)*. A ruler that follows the advice of the pious person *(brahmana)* never comes to grief. The *Vasishtha Smriti* states that the foremost duty of everybody is to have a chaste and lovable conduct (*acarah paramo dharmah sarveshamiti nishcayah* verse, 166).

Kautilya

Much has been said about Kautilya, the chief adviser of Emperor Chandragupta. It is no doubt clear that by the time Kautilya flourished Indian polity had undergone certain changes. The thoughtful and eternal policy in keeping with humanitarian interests had yielded place to narrow nationalistic interests. But despite this, we find in Kautilya a clear recognition of the fact that the ruler must be free from petty thoughts and narrow ideas. He must not indulge in unnecessary violence, and must not covet other's riches or women. According to Kautilya, a king's conduct must be free from falsehood and untruthfulness.[1]

What is the dominating note emanating from this discussion? It is clear that the Indians never wanted their rulers to be selfish and given to wars and conflicts. They accordingly taught a lesson of liberal-mindedness and universal love to the rulers. The ideal ruler of India is Rama who always tried to help the oppressed. Another ideal character is Krishna who did not spare his own relatives when they became corrupt. No doubt these two do not have any historical roots in the sense of modern history. But the influence wielded by these characters, even if they be legendary, shows that the Indian ideal of rulership followed this pattern. In fact even in the modern time Gandhi gave the concept of *Ramarajya*, a kingdom of love and universal sympathy, devoid of every type of exploitation and suppression.

The Indian ideal is to educate the rulers in such a manner that they may become the servants of society. This implies that a ruler should not instigate war, and try constantly to establish a region of peace and harmony on earth. The culmination of this ideal was once reached in the region of Ashoka. And this very culmination found its echo in the policy of *Panchasheel* enunciated by Jawaharlal Nehru.

The Hindus believe that the upper strata of human society has two births. It should be remembered that the lowest part of society is formed by the Shudras. But this social class is not a result of any heredity. It is the result of ignorance *(Ajnanatimirandhasya madyapana-ratasya ca rudhiram tena shudrannam vidhimantra vivarjitam) (Apastamba Smriti)*.

What are these two births? The first birth is the birth given by parents when a person is born in this world. But the second birth is given by the preceptor who initiates an individual into higher knowledge, and teaches him the lessons in moral discrimination and universal sympathy. This implies that a person is likely to be selfish and narrow-minded if he is allowed to have his natural growth. But if he is taught properly, he can grow into a true human being, a person endowed with rational judgement, and sound power of discrimination. Therefore, everybody needs a sound and right type of education, if he is to grow into an ideal citizen, and a rational human being. The old Indians, therefore, insisted upon a king to have a pious and learned adviser to guide him, to educate him, to show him the right path.

Tulasidas, the noted Hindi poet and thinker, has expressed the Indian ideal of a ruler very succinctly but suggestively in the following couplet:

Mukhiya mukha so chahiye, khana-pana me ek
Pale pose sakala anga, tulasi sahita viveka.

The leader should be like the mouth that eats and drinks, only to maintain all the bodily limbs with discrimination. The food eaten and the water drunk by mouth are used for the maintenance of the whole body.

As a ruler has a tendency to misuse power and authority bestowed upon him by society in his selfish interests, it is very necessary to educate him properly. In the absence of an effective and constructive education, a ruler shall develop into a tyrant, or a deceitful communist or socialist or a false democrat. The Indian thinkers, therefore, prescribed thorough education for the rulers. It is unfortunate that when degeneration took place, the ruler's post became hereditary and, therefore, in the course of time even the incompetent persons were able to take up the reins of a society. Naturally, they mismanaged the whole affair. The result was that the State contributed little in the progress of society and acted as an obstructing force. When society also plunged into ignorance, the State affairs became still worse. The result was that the enlightened India of the Vedic, and Puranic periods was lost into the thick of ignorance and ignorant and unenlightened rulers quarreled amongst themselves like mad dogs. They prized vain pride, and failed to honour discrimination. They plunged the society into uncalled-for wars and conflicts. The Rajputs who were brave by nature lacked the enlightened outlook due to the absence of an adequate education. Therefore they became an easy prey to the outside attacks, and ultimately India became enslaved. The story of the subjugation of India is a glittering example of how lack of education can be responsible for the ruin and downfall of even an old nation. Without education, the strength of a nation is thrown into wrong channel, and the bravery that should become a source of upliftment in fact becomes a tool of degradation, and the prosperity becomes disintegrated into innumerable pieces. Our modern world too shall be ruined if proper education is not given to the rulers. Our world, at present, is not different from the old nations. Because of the scientific inventions, the world has become one unit. If this fact is not realized and the elements of conflict are allowed to grow unchecked, nothing but annihilation awaits the world. Our modern world is bound to be one in this destruction, if it cannot become one in peace. There is no other alternative possible to our misconceived nationalistic standpoints.

The ideal of the ancient India was very illuminating on this point. The rulers realized their responsibilities well. They considered it to be their bounded duty to educate the prospective rulers properly. Tulasidasa gives ample expression to this healthy ancient Indian tradition when he writes that Rama, the ideal ruler as he was, not only loved his brothers well (along with his subjects), he taught his brothers lessons in ethical conduct in various ways. *(Rama karahi bhratan para priti: nana bhati sikhavahi niti: (Ramacharita Manasa, Uttarakhãnda).*

Panchatantra

The *Panchatantra* is a famous work of India. It is said that this work was composed by Vishnu Sharma to educate the princes. It is supposed to be the quintessence of the science of polity. It clearly warns that the position of a leader cannot be got easily. And if the leadership cannot rise to the occasion, it leaves every thing polluted. *(duraroham padam rajnam sarvaloke namaskritam svalpenapyapakarena brahmanyamiva dushyati. (Mitrabhedah,* 72)

It admits the difficulty that a true leader has to face. Such a person cannot side with a ruling power and hence is not liked by him; and if he works for the attainment of the interests of the ruling power, he cannot serve the public. Therefore, it is a rare phenomenon to find a really good leader (Panchatantra 142). It declares that virtuous conduct is the most desirable thing of life, and the essence of such a life is to render good to others and abstain from oppressing anybody *(paropakarah punyaya papaya parapidanam-Kakolukiyam,* v. 103). Non-violence is the most desirable virtue (*Panchatantra* 105-6). People who are divided are destroyed (*Panchatantra, A parikshitakarakam, v. 103*).

That leader who does not bring happiness to his followers and group properly is a useless creature *(prajam na ranjayed yastu raja rakshadibhirgunaih ajagalastanasyeva tasya janma nirarthakam).*

It emphasizes the point that if we do not find a good leader, society is bound to perish like a boat being destroyed in a deep sea *(yadi na syad narapati samyak neta tatah prajah akarnadhara jaladhau viplaveiteha nauriva).* And a proper leader, as we have seen, means a leader virtuous in conduct and protector of the people and an abstainer from violence and eager to render good to others.

It has been the firm faith of Indian thinkers that if the leaders lack the power of discrimination, they fail to find out what is good and what is bad in a particular situation: if they are unable to tread the path of universal well-being, they not only destroy themselves but even destroy the possibility of the development of virtuous conduct in the people constituting society *(avivekini bhupale nashyanti guninam gunah pravasarasike kante yatha sadhvyah stanonnatih).*

Hitopadesha, another famous treatise on polity, declares in unmistakable terms that a leader must possess virtuous conduct and be an adept in ethical behaviour *(dharmiko nitikushalah sah swami yujyate bhuvi).*

Sharangdharpaddhati declares that a leader must strive to make all the people of the world prosperous like the clouds of the rainy season *(parjanya iva bhutanamadharah prathavipatih).*

Kamandaki-Niti-sara declares that a leader can bring about prosperity in the world only when he seeks guidance from the enlightened elders *(rajasya jagato vridhderheturvridhadabhisangatah).*

It is clear, therefore, that the enlightened Indians always wanted leaders of society to adopt a constructive outlook on life and desist from any act whatsoever that would bring calamity and disaster to human society. Today when the world is being threatened with total annihilation due to the nuclear weapons, we must try to have in our midst such leaders as would be able to see this calamity before it actually overwhelms us, because a leader must be able to visualize the dangers before anybody else, and take steps to avoid the calamity *(anagatam yah kurute sa shochyate yo na karotyanagatam, Panchatantra, Kakolukiyam,* v. 227).

Wisdom lies in recognizing this fact that for the attainment of little gain in the form of a vain glory or a piece of territory or riches of another nation, let us not try to lose everything including our own lives and those of our near and dear, for all of us are equally exposed to the common danger posed by the nuclear weapons of annihilation *(na svalpasya krite bhuri nashayenmatimannarah, Panchatantra, Mitrabhedah,* v. 19).

A Clear Message

The message emanating from Indian Thought, therefore, is that a leader must be taught to respect human life and moral values. He must be so educated that he would not think of adopting a path leading human society towards grief and destruction. If we are unable to educate our leaders adequately we are sure to throw our human world in the cockpit of total annihilation. Let us be clear on this point.

This very constructive aspect of leadership was present in the modern Indian leaders of eminence like Gandhi, Nehru and others. Gandhi wrote about political power:

"To me political power is not an end but one of the means of enabling people to better their condition in every department of life. Political powers means capacity to regulate national life through national representatives. If national life becomes so perfect as to become self-regulated, no representation becomes necessary. There is then a state of enlightened anarchy. In such state every one is his own ruler. He rules himself in such a manner that he is never a hindrance to his neighbour."[2] A political leader must be taught this gospel before we accept him as our leader. In fact Gandhi gave this very type of advice to "An Indian Governor". "He must represent the best of all religions and all things Eastern or Western," writes Gandhiji "Being a citizen of India, he must be a citizen of the world. Thus simply, one reads, did the Khalif Omar, with millions of treasure at his feet, live; thus lived Janaka of ancient times; thus lived, as I saw him, the Master of Eton in his residence in the midst of, and surrounded by, the sons of the Lords and Nabobs of the British Isles". He adds:

"This does not pretend to be an exhaustive list of the virtues that an Indian Governor should represent. It is merely illustrative."[3]

It is clear from the above account that Gandhi did believe in the proper education of the rulers, because only then they can conform to the ideal set before them by Gandhiji.

The matter would be made still more clear by the following passage of Gandhiji:

"Indian must indeed have *Swaraj*, but she must have it by righteous methods. Our *Swaraj* must be real *Swaraj*, which cannot be attained by either violence or industrialization. India was once a golden land, because Indians then had a heart of gold. The land is still the same but is a desert because we are corrupt. It can become a land of gold again only if the base metal of our present national character is transmuted into gold. The philosopher's stone which can effect this transformation is a little word of two syllables—*Satya* (truth). If every Indian sticks to Truth, *Swaraj* will come to us of its own accord."[4]

Only leader who had developed a character can bring about the birth of people with character in a society. Hence the leader must be given adequate education so that right type of character is generated in him. Then the story of corruption shall not be heard in the domain of political activities.

Similar views were held by late Jawaharlal Nehru. Addressing the Services he had stated:

> "I appeal to all of them for integrity in the public services. This is not merely an ideal to be thought of or to be aimed at, but something which has to be practically achieved. It is intimately

connected with the individual good of all of us. Let our public services be a model of integrity and efficiency, of cooperation and courtesy."[5]

If integrity is so essential for a government officer, it is far more essential for a public leader. Surely integrity cannot be had in a person till we develop his character through a well-defined education. Nehru made the point quite clear by his followed declaration:

"We come back, therefore, to the question of standards and values and unless we have these, all the material good that we may achieve may lead to conflicts of the soul and disintegration of the social group."[6]

"What I am concerned with is not merely our material progress, but the quality and depth of our people. Gaining power through industrial processes, will they lose themselves in the quest of individual wealth and soft living? That would be tragedy, for that would be a negation of what India has stood for in the past and, I hope, in the present time also as exemplified by Gandhiji."[7]

Vinoba Bhave, a close associate of Gandhiji and his disciple, has clearly shown how important education is for social progress and for the production of leaders of character.

He says: "In the Upanishads we find that a student was not regarded as a *Snataka* (graduate) even after he had acquired all the learning unless he had actually fulfilled the aims of education in terms of being an inner development. Not only had he to be a master of letters but a master also of the will. He should be able to successfully observe his *Vratas* (pledged intentions) as an evidence of his mastery over himself. Like an able rider, he should be able to have full control over his body, sense and mind. . . . A student who has successfully passed this test proves to be really qualified for the effective service of his people. He alone becomes a good citizen and wherever he goes and whatever jobs he undertakes, he does so with confidence and courage."[8]

Ever to be Shunned

Vinoba is of the opinion that without proper education we cannot produce reliable and trustworthy political leaders too. Gandhiji had declared very emphatically that a virtuous conduct that is supposed to be very essential in the realm of religion is also very essential in the domain of politics:

> "For me, politics bereft of religion are absolute dirt, ever to be shunned. Politics concerns nations and that which concerns the welfare of nations must be one of the concerns of a man who is religiously inclined, in other words, a seeker after God and Truth. For me God and Truth are convertible terms, and if anyone told me that God was a God of untruth or a God of torture I would decline to worship Him. Therefore, in politics also we have to establish the Kingdom of Heaven."

Education alone can instill this much-needed morality into the mind of a person who is destined to tread the path of leadership and guide the destiny of countless people.

Dr. Radhakrishnan has stated in one of his speeches:

> "The future progress of the country depends on accomplishing in a few decades the work of centuries. The essential means of bringing about a new society is education. . . . In a Welfare State, our aim should be not only to provide the elementary necessities of food, clothing and shelter to all our citizens but to make them live as brothers even though they may belong to different races, creeds and provinces."

He proceeds to add:

> The cause of democracy is the cause of human individual, of the free spirit of man with its spontaneous inspiration and endeavour. Every man whose thoughts and feelings are not silted up has his own inner possession, which belongs to him alone, his holy shrine, which he has won for himself. When an individual is trained to appreciate his own holy being, he will develop a chastity of mind and spirit and approach with inner trembling another's sanctuary. Intoleration is basically unchastity. If we do not give this spiritual direction to our education, it fails in its purpose *(saksharo viprraritatve rakshaso bhavati dhruvam).*
> "Those who are learned but do not possess love, they really become

demoniac. They will be characterized by intellectual arrogance, spiritual crassness and coldness of heart."[9]

This observation of Dr. Radhakrishnan clearly points out how necessary it is to educate a leader. If he has no character, if he lacks a true perspective of human life, if he fails to imbibe the basic logic behind the institution of the State and puts a wrong example before the people, he is bound to lead the whole society to a wrong direction, and bring only degradation and defeat, misfortune and ruin to humanity.

Perhaps the Indian point of view of a leader has been aptly summed by Aurobindo Ghosh when he puts the ideal of a Superman before us. His concept of the Superman is quite distinct from that of Nietzsche.

His Supreman is Morality incarnate: "For, what is supermanhood but a certain divine and harmonious absolute of all that is essential in man? He is made in God's image, but there is this difference between the divine Reality and its human representative that every thing which in the one is unlimited, spontaneous, absolute, harmonious, self-possessed becomes in the other limited, relative, laboured discordant, deformed, possessed by struggle, kept by subservience to one's possessions lost by the transcience and insecurity which come from wrong holding." Aurobindo adds, "But in this constant imperfection there is always a craving and aspiration towards perfection. Man, limited, yearns to be the Infinite; relative is attracted in all things towards their absolute; artificial in nature, drives towards a higher ease, mastery and naturalness that must for ever be denied to her inconscient forces and half-conscient animals; full of discords, he insists upon harmony; possessed by nature and by her enslaved, is yet convinced of his mission to possess and master her. What he aspires to is the sign of what he may be. He has to pass by a sort of transmutation of the earthly metal he now is, out of flawed manhood into some higher symbol. For Man is Nature's great term of transition in which she grows conscious of her aim; in him she looks up from the animal with open eyes towards her divine ideal."

Education the Only Way

How a leader can rise to the height of the Superman? There is only one way, and that way is education. Only through the process of education we can transmute crude man into a chiselled image of a great ideal. And since we cannot do without leaders, we cannot do without their education. There may be some persons who by nature are educated in a true sense of the term. But a great number of leaders do not belong to this fine stock of humanity. They have to be given proper shape and personality before the responsibility of guiding the destiny of humanity is handed over to them.

Indian believed that the ruler must be a person following the noble path of truthfulness. He was called the leader of the people *(Prajapati)* and the *"prajapati"* is the follower of righteous conduct *(Satyadharma prajapati, Atharva Veda* 7.25.1). The *Atharva Veda* calls him a person who controls his senses and aims at the attainment of the spiritually highest ideal, at another place *(Acharyo brahmachari brahmachari prajapati,* AV 11.5.16). It was believed that a leader who cannot control his sensual tendencies is incapable of giving effective and efficient administration *(Brahmacaryanna tapasa raja rastram vi raksati,* (AV 11.5.16).

If the leader is not so highly gifted, how can he realize that the mother earth sustains the various languages, cultures, religions, etc. in a unified way like home? *(Janam vibhrati bahudha vivacasam nanadharmanam prthivi yathaukasam)* (AV 12.1.45).

How, moreover, he can realize that he must try to establish peace not only on the earth but even in the heavens and on the waters and see that the resources of nature are used for constructive and not destructive purposes? (*Yajur Veda* 36.17).

India has always believed that as are the leaders, so would be the followers *(yatha raja, tatha praja)*. Hence no nation, no society can afford to have uneducated rulers and leaders. The history of mankind bears brilliant testimony to the fact that whenever human society ignorantly accepted uneducated leaders as rulers, it had to suffer much in terms of loss of men, riches and the very progress of human society. Hence one must give second birth to the leaders through education so that they develop the capacity to discharge their duties properly.

We should be not surprised, therefore, if the wise teachers of India taught their disciples and the would-be leaders of their communities: "Speak truth. Follow righteous conduct. Make it a point to make good study. Do not swerve from truth. Do not swerve from morality. Do not swerve from aiming at real welfare. Do not swerve from attaining prosperity." (*Taittiriya Upanishad, anuvaka* 11).

Let us not forget that India never held two types of morality: one meant for the commoner and the other for the leaders. Krishnas and Sudamas were taught together to respect the tenets of human morality alike. The day the Indian thinkers (?) prescribed another standard of moral (?) code for the ruling class, the downfall of Indian community commenced. The real, original India never taught immorality in the name of morality. It always taught a leader to become a moral Superman as envisaged by Yogi Arvinda.

NOTES

1. Kautilya's *Artha Shastra*, Ch. 7, "Conduct of the Ideal Ruler".
2. *Young India*, 2.7.1931.
3. *Harijan*, 24.8.1947.
4. Gandhiji's Conclusion to his Paraphrase of *Unto This Last*, 63-64.
5. An Appeal to the Services, New Delhi, July 10, 1961.
6. Convocation Address at the University of Delhi, Dec. 6, 1958.
7. *India: Today and Tomorrow, Azad Memorial Lectures*, New Delhi, Feb. 22-23, 1959, published by the Indian Council for Cultural Relations.
8. Speech at Secunderabad, *Harijan*, 14.7.1951.
9. Dr. Radhakrishnan, Speech, March 3, 1954.

11

VOLTAIRE AND THE VEDAS

VOLTAIRE WAS the most notable thinker of the 18th century Europe. This celebrated thinker of France was against the ritualistic tendencies of religion much like the founder of the *Advaita, Shankara.* He declared:

> "The institution of religion exists only to keep mankind in order, and to make men merit the goodness of God by their virtue. Everything in a religion which does not tend towards this goal must be considered foreign or dangerous."

It appears that Voltaire was inspired by certain Indian scripture. Of course he himself was a free thinker. But the reading of Indian philosophical works gave him breadth of vision and liberality in outlook. Here are the words of Voltaire to prove that he was certainly acquainted with Hindu scripture:

> "What is this *Ezourveidam* which is in the King of France's library? It is an ancient commentary which an ancient Brahmin composed once upon a time, before the epoch of Alexander, on the ancient 'Veidam' which was itself much less ancient than the book of the 'Shasta'."
>
> "Let us respect, I tell you, all these ancient Indians. They invented the game of chess, and the Greeks went among them to learn geometry."
>
> "This *Ezourveidam* was lastly translated by a Brahmin correspondent of the unfortunate French India Company. It was brought to me on Mount Krapack, where I have long been observing the shows; and I sent it to the great Library of Paris, where it is better placed than in my home. Those who wish to consult it will see that after many revolutions produced by the Eternal, it pleased the Eternal to form a man who was called

> Adimo, and a woman whose name corresponds to that of life."
> "Is this Indian anecdote taken from the Jewish books? Have the Jews copied it from the Indians? Or can one say that both wrote it originally, and that fine minds meet?"
> "The Jews were not permitted to think that their writers had drawn anything from the Brahmins, for they had never heard of them. We are not permitted to think about Adam otherwise than the Jews. Consequently I hold my tongue, and I do not think at all."
> (Voltaire's *Philosophical Dictionary*, Carlton House, New York, p.125)

It is just possible that besides the *Yajur Veda* to which Voltaire has alluded, he may have studied some other Vedas or Upanishads or Puranas of the Hindus. But I have no doubt that Indian works did influence the mind of Voltaire which became consequently free from the usual sectarian bias present in the minds of the 18th century Europeans.

My inference about the great influence of Hindu scriptures becomes crystal clear from the following quotations from Voltaire's *Philosophical dictionary*:

> "Is it not probable that the Brahmins were the first legislators of the earth, the first philosophers, the first theologians?"
> "Do not the few monuments of ancient history which remain to us form a great presumption in their favour, since the first Greek philosophers sent to them to learn mathematics, and since the most ancient curiosities collected by the emperors of China are all Indian?"
> "One remarks a singular contrast between the sacred books of the Hebrews, and those of the Indians. The Indian books announce only peace and gentleness; they forbid the killing of animals; the Hebrew books speak only of killing, of the massacre of men and beasts; everything is slaughtered in the name of the Lord; it is quite another order of things."
> "It is incontestably from the Brahmins that we hold the idea of the fall of the celestial beings in revolt against the Sovereign of nature; and it is from there probably that the Greeks drew the fable of the Titans. It is there also that the Jews at last took the idea of the revolt of Lucifer, in the first century of our era. . . ."
> "Our missionaries have not failed to take this image of virtue for

that of the devil, and to assure us that the devil is worshipped in India. We have never been among these people but to enrich ourselves and to calumniate them."

Do we need any further proof to believe that Voltaire was impressed by the ancient Hindu thought and his liberal and humanitarian thinking was inspired by it?

12

INDIA AND THE PEACE IDEAL

THE QUESTION of world peace has assumed utmost importance in the modern period. Indian cultural thought is very important even from this standpoint. Let us try to see how far Indian thought can be called relevant in this direction.

When we think about peace, we have to begin from the dawn of Indian civilization. That means we should begin consideration of this topic right from the Vedic period. The Vedas are the earliest documents of the human race. "When the texts of the *Rig* and *Yajur* Vedas are completed", writes Wilson, "We shall be in the possession of materials sufficient for the safe appreciation of the results to be derived from them, and of the actual condition of the Hindus, both political and religious, at a date co-eval with that of the yet earliest known records of social organization – long enterior to the down of Grecian civilization prior to the oldest vestiges of the Assyrian Empire yet discovered – contemporary probably with the oldest Hebrew writings."[1] He adds: "The Vedas give us abundant information respecting all that is most interesting in the contemplation of antiquity."[2] The Veda comprises the works known as the four Vedic *Samhitas* or compilations of *Rig, Sama, Yajur* and *Atharva* together with supplementary and subsidiary works known as the Brahmanas, the works of rituals and the philosophical works known as the Aryanakas and the Upanishads.

The *Rig Veda* is definitely the most important of the four Vedas. According to Max Muller, "there is nothing more ancient than the hymns of the *Rig Veda*". The basic thought of the *Rig Veda* is that the entire world is but a manifestation of the Supreme. He desired to be many and the result was this creation *(Sa akamayata bahusyam prajayeya).* He, the One, desired that He would create the universe containing multifarious forms (*Rig Veda* X. 81.1). Again it is stated, "He the One wishing to be many inhibited His primary self, plunged in meditation, and evolved into the world of matter and mind, into both of which He entered". (RV 1.24.185) It was never doubted by the *Rig Veda* that there is only one God, one sole existent Truth. A query was put at the very outset as to which god deserves worship: *kasmai devaya avisha vidhema.* (RV 1.24.185) The conclusion that was drawn after a thorough logical consideration was that "the Real is One; the learned call It by different names, e.g. *Agni, Yama* and *Matarishva*". (RV 1.164.46) Our present object is limited. We do not intend to study the topic of the Real as discussed in the *Rig Veda.* We intend to study only the ideal of peace that emanates from it. Because of this faith that the entire universe is nothing but a manifested form of the Real, the Rig *Veda* maintained that the "life is immense" *(prano virat).*

The Nasadiya hymn declares that nature and spirit both are the aspects of the one Absolute. In the *Purusha Sukta* (X. 90) the basic unity of humanity has been symbolically stressed. "The Man had a thousand heads, a thousand eyes, a thousand feet. He covered the earth from all sides. . . . The Brahmin was His mouth, the Kshatriya was His arms, the Vaishya was His thigh, and the Sudra was His feet." What was suggested was the fact that the intellectuals, the rulers, the businessmen and the workers who constitute society are one as they are expressions of the Real. Just as for a healthy body, one needs harmony between the head, arms, stomach and feet, in the same way harmony is required in every class of society.

The *Rig Veda* considers *Rita* (moral principle) as the ruling law of society. It has to be obeyed by one and all. Otherwise there will be disorder and chaos in society. *Rita* is thus the universal essence of the things. It is the truth of the objects. Want of this principle is *An-rita* or falsehood (RV VII.56.12). Those who follow this universal principle of truth are good. Ordered conduct is termed a true *vrata. Vratani* should be understood as the ways of life of good men who follow the path of *Rita* (RV IX.121.1). *Varuna* has been depicted as the perfect example of the follower of *Rita* and is called *dhritavrata*, of unalterable ways.

The *Rig Veda* enjoins upon man to lead life under the very eye of God. He should be kind to all. Hospitability should always be practised. "The riches of one who gives do not diminish. . . . He, who possessed food, hardens his heart against the feeble man craving nourishment, against the sufferer coming to him for help and pursues his own enjoyment even before him, that man finds no consoler (RV VIII.6.5:1.2.6). Sorcery, witchcraft, seduction and adultery and condemned as vicious (RV VII.104.8:IV.5.5). Virtue is conformity to the law of God, which has love of man as its predominant note. "If we have sinned against the man who loves us, have ever wronged friend or comrade, have ever done an injury to a neighbour who ever dwelt with us or even to a stranger, O Lord, free us from the guilt of this trespass" (RV X.85.7).

The Vedic thought applies terms like *Rita* (moral principle), *Satya* (truth), *Sunrita* (bounty), *Sraddha* (faith) or *Dana* (charity) (RV X.117). This hymn can be considered as the earliest conception of religion as Social Service, enjoining upon man his first duty to feed the hungry as a gift of life, as hunger is a form of death. God worship is described at one place (RV VIII.79.2) as "clothing the naked, curing the sick, making the blind see, and the cripple walk about" thus equating God worship with social service. This very spirit is found pervading the description of *Shri Chandi* in the *Markandeya Purana* where offering worship to the Supreme dwelling in all creatures as the elemental principle of a Great Hunger *(ya devi sarva-bhuteshu kshudha-rupena samsthita)*.

The thought goes still further and declares that even those persons who are our enemies are not so, really speaking, and deserve our love and affection as they are also non-distinct from God. "Both Arya and Dasa belong equally to that glorious God to whom belongs the universe" (RV VIII.51.9). Even to commit any sin against any foreigner is bad and one ought to pray to God for forgiving such an unjust act (RV V.85.7).

The *Rig Veda* in its *Samajnana Sukta* (X.191) has very aptly paid adorations to the collective consciousness of the people, to which individual mind must pay its homage. Citizens are asked to come together to their Assembly *(samgachchadhvam)*, speak there with one voice *(samvadaddhavam)*, cultivating a union of minds *(sammanah)*, of hearts *(sahachittam)*, of policies *(samanamantrah)*, and of hopes and aspirations *(akuti)* and functioning in a common Assembly based on equality as an integral unity and not divided into groups and parties *(samitih samani)*. And then there is a call for equal sacrifice in the pursuit of a common policy (*samanam mantrah abhimantraye vah samanena vo havisha johomi* – call you to a common purpose which you serve with a common sacrifice). The ideal is that all should live in a pleasant harmony *(su-sahaasato)*. These ideals have a rare freshness and can be the eternal guides of humanity. The *Rig Veda* also makes a mention of the social institutions like Sabha and Samiti as the vehicles of these ideals. They are still the key terms of politics and social organizations.

"Twin Daughters of Prajapati"

The *Atharva Veda* (VII.12.1-2) has described *Sabha* and *Samiti* as "the twin daughters of *Prajapati*". The import of this statement is that the creative work for the society can be handled only through these agencies. They should function in unison *(samvidane)*. The *Atharva Veda* has given us a prayer for the integration of human hearts. The Prayer is addressed to the Diety designated as *Sammanasyam*, the Universal Mind, pervading, unifying and integrating individual minds (AV VI.60):

> "Let us all have a union of hearts *(sahridaya)*, of minds (sammanasya), without any ill-will *(avidvesha)*, with each loving the other as warmly as the cow its new-born calf *(anyah anyah abhiharshata aghnya jatam vasamiva)*. Let the son follow the ways of his father *(anuvrata)*, and be of one mind *(sammanah)* with his mother with whom he must not disagree. Let the wife speak to her husband honeyed words of sweetness *(madhumati)* and peace *(santivan vacham)*. Let not brother and sister bear ill-will towards each other. Let all speak words of gentleness, united in ideals and ways of life. Let the spread of *Brahma-Samjnana*, the knowledge of oneness of life, in every household, dispel discord and ill-will in every sphere, society, country and the whole world. Men's minds must thus be prepared for universal peace and brotherhood, for "wars begin in the minds of men". Let the people be not divided, but with pure heart work together in teams of cooperative effort, speaking with one another in agreeable words, with a common purpose and mind. Let all be of one purpose and mind under a common leadership in a spirit of fellowship. Let all have an equal share of water and food. Let all be yoked together in same harness for common work and worship like spokes revolving round the nave."

The *Yajur Veda* prays that the peace should prevail everywhere and "May I look upon everybody with an amount of friendliness" *(mitrasyaah chakshusha sarvani bhutani samikshe)*.

Thus there can be no doubt that the Vedic thought builds up an atmosphere of universal cordiality of humanity all round it. It advocates the establishment of Samghas or academies of learned men *(dhirah)* who are comrades *(sakha)* in culture and "who come together *(samyajante)* for developing the truths they had realized in their hearts *(krida tashteshu)* or reached by their minds *(manasho jabestu)* (RV X.71.8). The ideal of the Vedic thought was to cultivate knowledge, as only thereby the truth, the unity, can be grasped. That is why the prayer that is sung there is: "We meditate the excellent glory of *Savita*, the God, who inspireth us with knowledge." (YV III.35; RV III.62.10)

It was this torch of the spirit of universal brotherhood that was handed over by the Vedas to the Upanishads who enriched it all the more.

Love for Truth

In the Brahmanas too we find the spirit of high morality for the man duly preserved. Though these Brahmanas are full of rituals and lack the freshness and liberality of the Vedas, yet it must be conceded that the old spark of love for truth has not been forgotten. In the *Satapatha Brahmana* the sacrifice of all things *(sarva medna yajna)* is preached as a means to the attainment of spiritual freedom (XIII.7.1.1). The abandonment of the selfish shell is taught; the lofty ideal of the fulfilment of duties to gods, men and even to animals is tightly upheld. Truthfulness is an essential virtue which has to be absorbed in our life and behaviour; for otherwise, *Agni*, the lord of vows and *Vak*, and lord of speech shall be displeased (I.1.1.4; I.1.1.5; III.3.2.2., etc). Knowledge has been given due importance. "Yonder world", states the *Satapatha Brahmana* (X.5.4.15), "cannot be obtained by sacrificial gifts or by asceticism by the man who does not know this. That state belongs only to him who has this knowledge".

However, in the Upanishads we find the culmination of the human intelligence and wisdom. It is not only for the metaphysical insight that one should turn to the Upanishads. They should be consulted even otherwise for the solution of our secular problems for they, in the words of Dr. Radhakrishnan, try "to bring peace and freedom to the anxious human spirit".[3] (The Upanishads proclaimed to the man: "Thou art the sheath of *Brahman-Brahmanah koso'si-Tai Up.*). The entire world is due to the lustre of the Supreme and He resides in every heart, nay every thing, animate or inanimate. The entire life of a human being is a sacrifice. "The true sacrifice is man; his first 24 years are his morning libation . . . in hunger, in thirst, in abstinence from pleasure standeth his consecration. . . . In his eating and drinking and in his pleasures he keeps a holy festival and in his laughter and feasting and marrying he sings hymns of praise. Self-discipline, generosity, straightforwardness, *ahimsa* and truth in speech, these are his payments, and the bath of purification when the sacrifice is over is death" *(Chhandogya Upanishad III)*. What a lovely thought. The entire human life is worship of the Supreme. When one realizes this, nothing more is needed to understand. We are, really speaking, groping in the dark. That is why we fight, we forget the truth and feed our personality on shallow selfishness. Our only prayer, therefore, should be: "Lead me from the unreal to the real, lead me from darkness to light, lead me from death to immortality" *(Brihadaranyaka Upanishad* I.3.27). The *Chhandogya Upanishad* (VIII.3-12) has narrated a beautiful story for throwing light on the real nature of our Self. In fact the Upanishads make a mighty attempt to convince the world that the immortality (and peace and progress) cannot be attained if we cannot have the spirit of Maitreyi who declared: "What should I do with that by which I do not become immortal?" (Brih. Up. II.4.3). If we have that spirit then the Upanishads tell us in the language of Yajnavalkya: "Not for the sake of the beings are the beings dear but the beings are dear for the sake of the Self (Brih. Up. II.4.5). Our doctrines of socialism and communism and democracy cannot find any legitimate reason for propagation until and unless this basic stand is understood. One cannot strive for social service till one understands the ultimate nature of the Self. I should serve the humanity because, thereby, I serve Myself. If our concept of the Self is not clear then we cannot accept any social service as our ideal; for we do not know whether God exists, and beings are just individuals. Thus the only valid logic for our humanitarian attitude can be the Truth propounded by the Upanishads.

Thus we have to realize the supreme Truth and tell to everybody *"Tat Tvam asi"* – That art thou (Chhand. Up. VI.8.7). After grasping this truth everybody is bound to lose his petty self and feel that the real joy consists in becoming the limitless *(yo vai bhuma tat sukham, nalpe sukham asti)* (Chhand. Up. VII.23.1). We should definitely enjoy the life. But then we should do so in a non-attached manner without any shade of greed for anybody's riches (Isha Up. 1). Our effort should be to hear that is auspicious, to see what is auspicious (Prashna Up. Invocation).

Emphasis on Ethical Life

The Upanishads, therefore, rightly insist on the importance of ethical life (*Mundaka Upanishad* III.2.4; Brih. Up. IV.4.23). Human beings are free to act and it is their act which is responsible for their sorrow or happiness, decay or progress. "He fetters himself by himself, as a bird by its nest" declares the *Maitri Upanishad* (III.2). The fundamental virtues of human life are *dama* or self-restraint, *dana* or self-sacrifice, and daya or compassion (Brihad. Up. II). Self-restraint is very essential for a proper type of human life. If man is not to lead a beastly life, he must put a curb on his desires. *Dana* is, negatively speaking, freedom from greed and positively speaking assistance to those who need. Daya does not mean mere absence of cruelty. It means leaving discord and be at peace with all. The Upanishadic outlook has no place for any narrowness. *Satyakama* of unknown origin was despised but was given the highest truth; Gargi, though a woman, was deeply respected; Ajatshatru, King Asvapati Kaikeya though Kshatriya were revered for their knowledge.

Thus we find that the Vedic thought has a very profound outlook. It gives us that spirit with which we must look at the world if we are to seek happiness. The *Yajur Veda* has rightly stated: "The Veda with its words of supreme good *(vacham kalyanim)* must be taught to the people at large *(janebhyah)*, to Brahmin and Kshatriya, to Shudra and Vaishya, to one's own people and, even to foreigners." (XXV.2). The entire world can profit by these teachings as they aim at universal peace.

The *Smriti* literature of India too says the same thing. Manu, the supreme law-giver of India, has enjoined upon people to seek light from their reason *(manah putam samacharet,* VI.46). The *Bhagavadgita* declares that God exists in all beings and hence the social service is the best worship of God (VI.30, 31). "He who looks upon all as one, on the analogy of his own self, and looks upon the pleasure and pain of all with a similar eye, such a Yogi is regarded as supreme" (BG VI.32). The *Mahabharata* delcares in this very strain, "Whatever is not conducive to social welfare, or what ye are likely to be ashamed of doing, never do" (*Shanti Parva*, 124.66). And lest one should have confusion, the best way is to follow the conduct of great persons *(mahajano yena gatah sa pathah, Vana Parva* 312.115).

The teaching of the Mahabharata is very clear: the Self is like a river, self-restraint is a place of pilgrimage, truth is water, moral conduct banks and compassion ripples. One should take path in such an auspicious river.

This clearly indicates that the ancient Hindu thought advocates an ideal of universal peace and prosperity.

The Bhagavata Purana declares that it is our "animal intelligence" *(pashu buddhi)* which prompts us to differentiate between different individuals and nations. (VII.5.12) Prahlada teaches a gospel of universal love and compassion. (VII.6.24) The Indian ideal is that even salvation is not to be sought individually. Till all are happy and healthy, a wise person cannot feel satisfied. (VII.9.44)

We have seen hereinabove that the Indian thought aims at universal peace and brotherhood.

This spirit of brotherhood and peace is found in all the religions and schools that emanated on the soil of India. Let it be added here that this peace ideal was never supposed as unpractical. We learn from the Bauddha Jatakas that the Gautama, the Enlightened, tried to dissolve a dispute between two kingdoms of Kauliya and Kapilavastu by pointing to the fighters that to wage wars for settlements of disputes is simply foolish and barbarian. The two kingdoms were just beginning their conflict on the issue of the use of the water of the river Rohini. The Buddha prevailed upon them to ponder over the fact that invaluable human life was going to be wasted for a petty thing like water which can be had without any price. This secret lies in the heart of every event that leads two factions of the humanity to fight. Land, riches, woman, etc., are valueless as compared to the value of human life and yet the men fight like bulldogs for these petty things. To call this attitude "humanitarian nonsense" is to admit our weakness for clear and straightforward thinking.

That it is possible to maintain peace and order in a nation even without taking recourse to violence and threats was demonstrated very eloquently by the greatest emperor of India, viz. Ashoka. He clearly declared: "There is no higher duty than the welfare of the whole world. And what little effort I make is in order that I may be free from debt to the creatures, that I may"[4] render them happy *here* and they may gain heaven in the next world. "In Kalinga Edicts he tells us that just as for his offspring he desires welfare and happiness, pertaining not only to this world but also the next, he desires it precisely for all mankind – sava-munisa.[5] H.G. Wells has rightly honoured Ashoka by calling him the greatest Emperor of the world. "Amidst the tens and thousands of names of monarchs that crowd the columns of history", states Wells, "their majesties and graciousness and serenities and royal highnesses and the like, the name of Ashoka shines and shines almost alone as a star. From the Volga to Japan his name is still honoured. China, Tibet, and even India, though it has left his doctrine, preserve the tradition of his greatness. More living men cherish his memory today than have ever heard the names of Constantine or Charlemagne.[6]

Ashoka thus typifies the true Indian ideal of world brotherhood and human prosperity to a large extent. However, it is not the place to trace any history of India. Our aim is only to acquaint ourselves with those basic voices of India which spoke emphatically for the adoption of the ideal of world peace and the progress of the humanity. This brings us to Gandhi, the Great Soul.

World State Must Evolve

Before, however, we take up the views of Gandhi, it may be quoted what Shri Aurobindo, who is more famous as philosopher than as a political thinker, has said: "In the conditions of the world at present, even taking into consideration its most disparaging features and dangerous possibilities, there is nothing that need alter the view we have taken of the necessity and inevitability of some kind of world union; the drive of nature and the compulsion of circumstances and the present and future need of mankind make it inevitable. The general conclusions we have arrived at will stand and the consideration of the modalities and possible forms or lines of alternative or successive development it may take. The ultimate result must be the formation of a World State and the most desirable form it would be a federation of free nationalities in which all subjection or forced inequality and subordination of one to another would have disappeared and, though some might preserve a greater natural influence, all would have an equal status. A confederacy would give the greatest freedom to the nations constituting the World State, but this might give too much room for fissiparous or centrifugal tendencies to operate; a federal order would then be the most desirable. All else would be determined by the course of events and by general agreement or the shape given by the ideas and necessities that may grow up in future. A world union of this kind would have the greatest chances of long survival or permanent existence."[7]

The fact is that every thinker of India who had drunk the nectar of the Indian Thought had a zeal for world peace and common human progress. Therefore one should not be surprised at the rise of Gandhi in India. Gandhi brought the craving for human peace in a very passionate manner. He very boldly declared that non-violence is the only way befitting the dignity of human beings. "Non-violence is the law of our species as violence is the law of the brute. The spirit lies dormant in the brute, and he knows no law but that of physical might. The dignity of man requires obedience to a higher law – to the strength of the spirit."[8] Gandhi hated war – the violent war. He condemned it for the various reasons. War takes "so many lives"; moral loss is greater still; lying and deception which destroy soul are perfected; sexual morality collapses; a man becomes a brute. He declared, "The way of peace is the way of truth".[9] "I know that war is wrong, is an unmitigated evil". "Peace is unattainable by part performance of conditions, even as chemical combination is impossible without complete fulfilment of conditions of attainment thereof."[10]

Gandhiji had pleaded for a religious outlook. Once a question was put to him what his motive in life was, whether it was religious or social or political. And his reply was: "Purely religious. This was the question asked me by the late Mr. Montangue when I accompanied a deputation which was purely political. 'How have you, a social reformer', he exclaimed, 'found your way into this crowd?' My reply was that it was only an extension of my social activity. I could not be leading a religious life unless I identified myself with the whole of mankind, and that I could not do unless I took part in politics. The whole gamut of man's activities today constitutes an indivisible whole. You cannot divide social, economic, political and purely religious work into watertight compartments. I do not know any religion apart from human activity. It provides a moral basis to all other activities which they would otherwise lack, reducing life to a maze of 'sound and fury signifying nothing'."[11]

Gandhiji believed in the fact that the entire world is permeated by the Supreme God *(Isavasyamidam sarvam)*. Gandhiji interpreted it in his own way and stated that socialism and even communism is implicit in this mantra.[12] It implies a way of universal peace and good of all living beings. Gandhiji interpreted history in spiritual terms and believed that "man is by nature going higher".

Fundamentally Good

There can be no doubt that Gandhi tried to give new twist to our approaches in society and politics. We started from the basic idea that man is ignoble, he is a brute. Gandhi told us that man is fundamentally good. We think that war is inevitable and the conflicts can be resolved only by bloody warfares. Gandhi told us that disputes can be solved in a much better way if we have a spirit of non-violence. We thought that men are different while Gandhi told us that men are spiritually one and hence we ought to love everybody. Peace should characterize our conduct. We thought that religion must be discarded from politics; Gandhi stated that it should form our essential background of our personality. We thought that the State is a permanent institution, while Gandhi said that it is a passing phase. What is most important is that we thought man can be made ideal by the State laws, while Gandhi stated that man has to make his personality sublime himself. Thus Gandhi gave us the gospel of universal love and affection. He preached the cultivation of a non-attached outlook for leading a sane human life. These are the rudiments of a new creation of mankind. The old habits have to be discarded if new ideals have to be cherished.

For the proper appreciation of the Sarvodaya ideal, pleaded by Gandhi,[13] we should try to understand the concept in some detail. His lucid analysis of Sarvodaya was as follows:

1. That the good of the individual is contained in the good of all.
2. That a lawyer's work has the same value as the barber's in as much as all have the same right of earning their livelihood from their work.
3. That a life of labour, i.e. the life of the tiller of the soil and the handicraftsman is the life worth living.

The first principle establishes the most intimate relationship between the individual and society as a whole. The second principle proves that the material worth of every kind of labour should be the same. It follows, therefore, that there should be no inequity between the earnings of two persons. The third principle gives us that fundamental secret which underlies every kind of happiness. Its absence is the cause of the various types of conflicts and wars. The world shall not be a place of wars and devastations if we just become moderate in our aspirations. These three principles are the supreme principles of the Gandhian Sarvodaya and are undoubtedly the cornerstone of the human ideal of peace and happiness. Gandhiji rightly disagreed with the utilitarian ideal of the greatest good of the greatest number which ethically does not go very far. According to Gandhiji "it means in its nakedness that in order to achieve the supposed good of 51 per cent the interest of 49 per cent may be, or rather, should be sacrificed. It is a heartless doctrine and has done harm to humanity. The only real, dignified, human doctrine is the greatest good of all, and this can be achieved only by greatest self-sacrifice." This doctrine was based on the well-known Indian ideal of *sarvabhutahitaya*, i.e. for the betterment of all.[14] The famous *Isha Upanishad* states in its very first shloka: "God the Ruler pervades all that exists in this Universe. Therefore, renounce and dedicate all to Him, and then enjoy or use the portion that may fall to thy lot. Never covet anybody's possessions".

Naturally this Sarvodaya aims at the establishment of a classless society. Gandhiji explained this in his writings.[15] Marx also aims at that classless structure of society. But while for Marx the attainment of such an ideal is something impossible, for Gandhiji such a classless pattern of society can be seen to be a great possibility. The reason is that while Marx pins his faith on violence for bringing about change in society Gandhiji advocates peaceful ways of *satyagraha* and *ahimsa* for bringing about transformation of the social order. It is psychologically impossible to attain peace by the sword. Violence shall breed only violence. Hence the Marxian ideal of classless society is nothing more than a sweet theoretical dream. If at all any classless society were to descend on this earth, it will be possible only by the way Gandhiji has advocated. He wrote[16] very clearly that the differences between man and man cannot be destroyed with a sword. The sword only cuts a body. What is needed is to transform the heart. And transformation of heart is not brought about by such violent measures.

Peace in Four Phases

Without going into further details, we may forthwith come to the question of peace. Gandhiji's *Sarvodaya* ideal included all people and all the nations irrespective of caste, creed, colour, sex, etc. he stated: "I believe in the absolute oneness of God, and, therefore, also of humanity. What though we have different bodies? We have but one soul. The rays of the sun are many through refraction. But they have the same source. I cannot, therefore, detach myself from the wickedst soul, nor may I be denied identity with the most virtuous. . . . If we are the sons of the same God and partake of the same divine essence, we must partake of the sin of every person, whether he belongs to us or to another race."[17] Gandhiji, therefore, was a great prophet of peace. He hated war and conflict and never advocated violence even in the face of the great possible provocations. He tried to achieve peace in four phases: ideological, social, political and economic.

The Ideological Phase is very clear to everybody. Throughout his life he advocated universal love and peaceful methods to attain any objective. In 1938 he advocated the enlistment of volunteers for the formation of Shanti Senas or Peace Brigades in cities and villages to combat communal riots. In the same year he toured the North Western Frontier Province and addressed the *Khudai Khidmatgars*, i.e. non-violent Red Shirts. In his addresses Gandhiji described "in minute details the nature and working of Non-Violence".[18] His concept of *Swaraja* too was unique. Though he fought throughout his life most heroically for the liberation of India and establishment of *Swaraja*, the *Swaraja* "was synanymous with *Rama Rajya*, the establishment of the Kingdom of Righteousness on earth".[19] Thus he never pleaded for any narrow nationalism. His *Swarajya* was a "sovereignty of the people based on pure moral authority".[20]

The Social Phase of Peace was characterized by the organization of Harijana Sevaka Sangh in September, 1932. He founded it to remove by peaceful means the difficulties and disabilities of the Harijans. The Hindustani Talim Sangh was started by him in 1937 for initiating education based on non-violence. He declared at that time, "All our problems have to be solved non-violently. Our arithmetic, our science, our history will have non-violent approach and the problems in these subjects will be coloured by non-violence"[21] The Kasturba Gandhi Memorial Trust (1946), meant for the upliftment of womenfolk by non-violent means, and the Hindustani Prachar Sabha (1942) meant for giving a unifying language can also be mentioned here.

The Political Phase of Peace of Gandhi earned him a world-wide recognition. Here was a man who fought with bare hands against the mightiest empire of the World History. His method was non-violence and *Satyagraha*. He infused new courage in the masses of the nation that was under the yoke of slavery for thousands of years and which was timid and depressed. Gandhiji not only waged this unique struggle, he bravely won or snatched liberty from a very cruel and well-armed hand. The most beautiful aspect of the case is that despite this struggle the goodwill and cordiality was not lost between the parties. There is then the Economic Phase of Peace. The Ahmedabad Textile Labour Association (1920), Rashtriya Mazdoor Congress (1947) All India Spinners' Association (1925), The All India Village Industries

Association (1935), etc. were the instruments of founding peace in the Economic Phase.

Gandhiji's nationalism was a big medium of serving the vast humanity. "My notion of *Purna Swaraja* is not isolated independence but healthy and dignified inter-dependence", declared Gandhiji.[22] He stated on another occasion, "Through *Swaraja*, we would serve the world".[23] He went still further and said that he "would like to see India free and strong, so that she may offer herself as a willing and pure sacrifice for the betterment of the world.[24]

Gandhiji was an out and out peace-lover. He was a staunch moralist in his objective and means. He quoted[25] appreciatively the *shloka* from the *Mahabharata* saying:

"With hands upraised I cry;
But none listens to me;
Dharma yields both wealth and desire;
Why is that Dharma not observed?

We find thus that Gandhiji is a massive champion of peace – peace not only in our actions but even in our thoughts. The truth is that, first of all, we must free our minds from hatred and violence, only then peace can be achieved in our actions. We must not think that the sublimity of an ideal can justify the use of any unfair means for obtaining it. "Destructive means employed engender corresponding counter-means and so forth ad infinitum. As the Buddha put it: "If hatred responds to hatred, when and where will hatred end?"[26] "Our personal experience and the study of history", states Aldous Huxley, "make it abundantly clear that the means whereby we try to achieve something are at least as important as the end we wish to attain. Indeed, they are seen more important."[27] Gandhiji was, therefore, quite right in thinking that "means and ends are convertible terms."[28] If we desire peace, our means should be equally peaceful. Hence the Gandhian instruments of Truth, Non-violence, Self-purification and Satyagraha are capable of attaining their objective of peace. While Marxian ideal of classless society shall remain only a wishful thinking. "In the final state," Observes Gandhiji, "therefore, there is no political power, because there is no State".[29] Gandhiji could say so because at that phase the individuals would become perfectly moral human beings. But the members of the Marxian society, brought up as they are in the class-war doctrine, shall find it hard to keep peace. We can conclude, therefore, that in the contemporary world where man-killing weapons have been perfected to a terrific extent, the Gandhian way is a robust message for the crisis-ridden humanity all over the world.

We have studied hereinabove the basic currents of the Indian philosophy and have seen how it has exercised its sway over the minds of the Indian thinkers even in the realm of politics. Because of its Vedantic outlook, from the very beginning of her history, India had a universality of outlook. The *Rig Veda* delcares: "The loving sage beholds that mysterious Reality wherein the universe comes to have one home" *(venas tat pashyan nihitam guha sad yatra vushvam bhavaty eka-nidam).* All men are brothers and all the three worlds are our native places *(bhrataro manujah serve svadesho bhuvana-trayam).* Manu enjoined on the Indians to shape their conduct in such a way that it may be worthy of imitation by all in the world:

etad desha prasutasya sakashad agra-janmanah
swam swam caritrum shiksheran prathviyam sarvamnavah.

The ideal that was placed before the Indians was that for the noble-hearted people the entire world is one family *(udarcharitanam vasudhaiva kutumbakam).*

India has upheld the tradition of peace by not attacking any other nation in her history.

We find thus that "the search after the universal is the one search of Indian philosophy and religion".[30] For the Indians the "brotherhood already exists; only there are some persons who fail to see this".[31] Nay, India philosophy goes still further and declares that a single reality is pervading the universe. "Vedant formulates not universal brotherhood, but universal oneness".[32] Hence it is very easy and natural for the true Indian to feel that "I belong as much to India as to the world".[33] That is why Tulasidas has declared that only that wealth is good which serves all *(kirati bhanati bhuti bhali soisursarisam sab kanh hit hoi). He repeatedly declares that those who wish the happiness of all, for them everything is attainable (par hit bas jinhake man mahi-tinh kanh jag durlabh kachu nahi).* This outlook follows automatically if one were to see God everywhere and worship him accordingly *(Siya Ram maya sab jag jani-karanhu pranam jori jag nahi).* The *Shvetashvataropanishad* has declared as follows:

1. *sahah navavatu* – may we be able to protect each other.

2. *saha nau bhunaktu* – may we enjoy the wealth of the world conjointly.
3. *saha virya karvavahai* – may we show prowess conjointly.
4. *tejaswinavadhitamastu* – may we be full of splendour.
5. *ma vidvidhavahai* – may we not be jealous of each other.

In one word, we should see the world with friendly eyes (*mitrasya cakshusha samikshamane*).

We find thus that the Indian thought is one of the betterment of all; may all cross the difficulties.

Some thinkers whom we have considered have clearly and specifically tried to assert the basic unity of the humanity. As a matter of fact all truly cultured Indians whether their names have been mentioned or not have upheld this ideal of universal brotherhood. If we want to summarize the basic attitude of the Indian philosophy applied in the realm of social relations, we can state safely that it is contained in the SARVODAYA ideal as enunciated by Gandhiji. That ideal is the fruition of Indian thought. It aims at peace and progress of every member of society of human beings by non-violent means. Sarvodaya ideal is that Indian ideal which shows the path of peace for the entire universe. There is nothing better than man *(nahi manushat sresthataram hi kinchit)*. So let us build an ideal world of true human beings whose knowledge shall give them a broad outlook *(sa vidya ya vimuktaye)* and who shall aspire to create a kingdom of universal love and affection and destroy everything that puts any obstruction in the attainment of this objective.

NOTES

1. *Journal of the Royal Asiatic Society*, Vol. 13, 1852, p.206.
2. ibid.
3. *Indian Philosophy*, Vol. I, p.138.
4. *Rock Edict VI-Ashoka* by D.R. Bhandarkar, p.199.
5. ibid. p.202.
6. *An Outline of History*, p.212.
7. *The Ideal of Human Unity*.
8. Non-violence in Peace, Vol. I, p.2.
9. ibid. p.57.
10. ibid. p.116.
11. ibid. p.171.
12. *Harijan*, 2.2.1937.
13. *Sarvodaya* (Hindi), pp.3-4.

14. Nava-Jivana (Hindi), 9.12.1926.
15. *Harijan*, 18.1.1948.
16. *Harijan Sevaka*, 20.3.1937.
17. *Great Soul*, by Herrymon Maurev, p.41.
18. *Young India*, 9.12.1926.
19. ibid., 4.5.1921.
20. *Harijan* 2.1.1937.
21. ibid., 7.5.1938.
22. *Young India*, 26.3.1931.
23. ibid., 16.4.1931.
24. ibid., 17.9.1925.
25. *Harijan*, 13.7.1940.
26. Keyserling, *Mahatma Gandhi*, edited by Dr. Radhakrishnan, pp.184-5.
27. *Ends and Means*, p.52.
28. *Young India*, 26.12.1924.
29. ibid., 2.7.1931.
30. *Complete Works of Vivekananda*, Vol. III, p.81.
31. ibid., p.365.
32. ibid., p.129.
33. ibid., Vol. V, p.67.

13

AUROBINDO AND THE RELIGION OF HUMANITY

RELIGION IS as old as man. But the concept of religion has no uniformity. In the absence of any uniform concept of religion, it is desirable to get some insight as to its nature from its etymological meaning. The term religion is derived from the Latin term *"religare"* meaning "to bind". Hence, religion is essentially a binding force. The *Chamber's Twentieth Century Dictionary* has accepted the term *"religion"* in the sense of "belief in, recognition of, or an awakened sense of, a higher unseen controlling power or powers, with the emotion and morality connected therewith".

Everything in this world is subject to change. There is no exception to this rule. In the olden period religion was generally ritualistic in nature. It cannot be said that ritualism has entirely faded away from religion in the modern period, but it can be said without any hesitation that a modern intellectual has discarded ritualism. Old gods have been discarded and humanity has taken their place. This change in the domain of religion is in keeping with the revolutionary changes that have taken place in the history of mankind.

It does not, however, mean that every human being has started worshipping humanity. Individual minds have their stages of evolution. Aurobindo has rightly stated, "The ghosts of things dead are very troublesome actualities and they now abound – ghosts of dead religions, dead arts, dead moralities, dead political theories, which still claim either to keep their rotting bodies or to animate partly the existing body of things. Repeating obstinately their sacred formulas of the past, they hypnotize backward-looking minds and daunt even the progressive portion of humanity".[1]

But the concept of the religion of humanity is slowly but steadily gaining ground. It has to be added that the nature of this religion of humanity has not crystallized so far. To quote the words of Aurobindo, it "may be either an intellectual and sentimental ideal, a living dogma with intellectual, psychological and practical effects, or else a spiritual aspiration and rule of living, and partly the sign, partly the cause of a change of soul in humanity".[2]

The concept of the religion of humanity was put forth for the first time in the West in the 19th century. According to Aurobindo, it is "the *manasa putra* of the rationalist thinkers, who brought it forward as a substitute for the formal spiritualism of ecclesiastical Christianity". and, "It tried to give itself a body in Positivism, which was an attempt to formulate the dogmas of this religion, but on too heavily and severely rationalistic a basis for acceptance even by an Age of Reason".[3] He is of the opinion that humanitarianism, philanthropy, social service, etc., are merely the outward expression of this very religion of humanity. Not only this, even democracy, socialism, pacifism "are to a great extent its hyproduct or at least owe much of their vigour to its presence".[4] The fundamental gospel of this religion is that "mankind is the godhead to be worshipped and served by man". A follower of this religion must try to abandon the lesser gods like nationalism, the Church, the State, or narrow-minded religion. It is not that these objects are totally rejected. What is done is that they are considered inferior to humanity, and if there is any conflict between humanity and these ideals, humanity-ideal must win. Well-being of mankind is the sole objective to be attained. In the inimitable words of Aurobindo, "No injunctions of old creeds, religions, political, social, or cultural, are valid when they go against its claims".[5] Even science, which occupies such an important position in the modern age, is to be considered valuable only so far as it serves humanity. If it goes against the interests of humanity, it must be rejected without any hesitation. This new religion abhors war, capital punishment, cruelties of all kinds, whether committed by an individual, the State or community. The oppression and exploitation of man by man, of class by class, of nation by nation, in any garb, which have been sanctioned by old traditions and religions, must be stopped, nay, eradicated. This religion proclaims "Man must be sacred to man, regardless of all distinctions of race, creed, colour, nationality, status, political or social advancement".

The Ideal and the Spirit

Man has to be protected against disease, oppression, cruelty, penury and lack of security. "The life of man has to be held sacred, preserved, strengthened, ennobled, uplifted. This new religion demands that even the mind and the heart of man have to be protected from every kind of violence and given freedom to expand in the right direction. Their development, however, should be so directed that their powers are yoked for the service of humanity. As is clear, noble sentiments alone are not sufficient. They must be "given full and practical recognition in the persons of man and nations and mankind." This is the ideal and spirit of this religion, which can be termed "the intellectual religion of humanity".

This religion of humanity is surely a great advancement over the past religions which incited people to fights hundred years' war and unleash a torrent of physical torture and violence on their so-called opponents. This religion gets appreciation of Aurobindo in the following words:

> "It accomplished rapidly many things which orthodox religion failed to do effectively, largely because it acted as a constant intellectual and critical solvent, an unsparing assailant of the thing that is and an unflinching champion of the things to be, faithful always to the future, while orthodox religion allied itself with the powers of the present, even of the past, bound itself by its pact with them and could act only at best as a moderating but not as a reforming force. Moreover, this religion has faith in humanity and its earthly future and can therefore aid its earthly progress, while the orthodox religions looked with eyes of pious sorrow and gloom on the earthly life of man and were very ready to bid him bear peacefully and contentedly, even to welcome its crudities, cruelties, oppressions, tribulations as a means for learning to appreciate and for earning the better life which will be given us hereafter."[6]

The merit of this new religion has to be accepted. It has humanized society, humanized law and punishment, humanized the outlook of man on man, abolished legalized torture and the cruder forms of slavery, raised those who were depressed and fallen, gave large hopes to humanity, stimulated philanthropy and charity and the service of mankind, encouraged everywhere the desire of freedom, put a curb on oppression and greatly minimized its more brutal expressions. Aurobindo thinks that it has succeeded in "humanizing war and would have succeeded entirely but for the contrary trend of modern science". Thanks to this religion, for it has made it possible for man to conceive of a world free from war as imaginable "even without waiting for the Christian millennium". We should not forget that prior to the dawn of this religion "peace was a rare interlude of constant war". Due to the influence of this religion now war has become an interlude.

Now the world has new conceptions of the dignity of the human being. Man, for the first time in human history, has been given some importance. That is why the distinctions of the serf and the master, owner and the labourer, the rich and the poor are thinning down. We have new ideas about education and development of human personality. Our old ideals of supermen trampling their fellow beings have been thrown away. Now we seriously think about striking off the distinctions between man and man on the basis of riches or status. Democracy. Communism and such other noble social and political ideals have been accepted throughout the world. To talk about imperialism and dictatorship is to lower ourselves in the eyes of our fellow beings in these days. It cannot be denied that at least theoretically a brighter image of a human being has emerged in the modern age as compared with past periods of human history.

Egoism the Obstacle

So far we have talked about the achievement of the new religion of humanity. But every true religion has to be founded on the actual conduct of its followers. We have to accept that the religion of humanity is not reflected in the conduct of most of its adherents. The new religion "has to make itself more explicit, insistent and categorically imperative". We must try to analyse the cause of the contrary conduct of the acceptors of this religion. Our analysis reveals that human egoism is the main cause. According to Aurobindo, this egoism is "the enemy of all real religions". Egoism of individual, egoism of class, egoism of nation – there are these three forms of egoism, which do not allow this new religion to prosper.[7] Unless this egoism is mastered, no progress can be attained. This egoism is so strong that it cannot be eliminated easily. But if efforts are made, it can be softened.

For the attainment of the objective of religion of humanity it is absolutely essential that the egoism is tamed. Although the religion of humanity appears to be new to the people of the West, so far as we Indians are concerned, it is not new. According to Aurobindo, this religion has drawn inspiration from the Vedic injunction of human unity. The basic teaching of Indian philosophy is to underline the unity of mankind. The *Bhagavadgita* states emphatically that the Lord is present in everything. The Supreme is present even in the most lowly and undeveloped beings.[8] Aurobindo points out that the outward, formal and mechanical political changes are incapable of leading humanity to its aim. Real progress is attainable only when we have "perfected and developed human nature". He is of the opinion that at present religion of humanism is "a purely intellectual and sentimental religion". And, "The intellect and the feelings are merely instruments of the being and they may be the instruments of either its lower external form or of the inner and higher man, servants of the ego or channels of the soul. If the new religion intends to get success, it must seek its spiritual base. The grand ideals of liberty, equality and fraternity that were born in Europe in the 18th century still remain unattained. The liberty has been confused with "an outward and mechanical and unreal liberty", the equality has been conceived in an "equally outward and mechanical" sense, and fraternity has been misconceived as the "outward and mechanical principle of equal association or at best a comradeship of labour".

An explanation of this confusion has been provided by Aurobindo: "This is because the idea of humanity has been obliged in an intellectual age to mask its true character of a religion and a thing of the soul and the spirit and to appeal to the vital and physical mind of man rather than his inner being. It has limited his effort to the attempt to revolutionize political and social institutions and to bring about such a modification of the ideas and sentiments of the common mind of mankind as would make these institutions practicable; it has worked at the machinery of human life and on the outer mind much more than upon the soul of the race."[9] Aurobindo is of the opinion that the political, legal and social revolutions that are aims of the religion of humanity cannot be achieved unless they are based on "a change of the inner human nature and inner way of living". If we desire to achieve the higher ideals of freedom, equality and brotherhood, we must destroy "the individual and the communal ego". Unless this ego is destroyed, the equality that we shall get, shall be artificial, liberty shall be a mere competitive individualism, because "the ego to speak of fraternity is for it to speak of something contrary to its nature". The common egoistic ends can give us exploitation in some new and dangerous form.

Humanity has Gained Nothing

Brotherhood is the key principle which can give us a world untouched by exploitation and corruption. But this brotherhood can exist only in the soul. "It can exist by nothing else." The three principles of freedom, equality and unity are, really speaking, "the eternal attributes of the Spirit". Aurobindo is quite right. The objective of religion[10] can be attained only on the acceptance of the spirit. Denial of spirit has reduced Communism to some kind of dictatorship, and it has reduced democracy to a rule of opportunists. Humanity has gained nothing substantially. The essence of the Advaitic teaching is that the Brahman alone is the sole reality and the universe is a manifestation of that Supreme and not an outcome of inert matter. This view has been substantiated by the modern science too, which finds a dance of energy in the universe instead of any immobile matter. This is clear from the words of Capra,

> "Atoms consist of particles and these particles are not made of any material stuff. When we observe them, we never see any substance; what we observe are dynamic patterns continually changing into one another – a continuous dance of energy."[11]

NOTES

1. Shri Aurobindo International Centre of Education Collection, Vol. IX, Shri Aurobindo Ashrama, Pondicherry, 1962, 756.
2. ibid.
3. ibid., p.757.
4. ibid.
5. ibid.
6. ibid., p.759.
7. ibid., p.761.
8. *The Bhagvadgita*, VI-30, VII-7.
9. op. cit., p.763.
10. op. cit., p.764.
11. Capra, F., *The Tao of Physics*, Collins Books, p.274.

INDEX